Embracing the Rainbow

Published by
BRIDGER HOUSE PUBLISHERS, INC
P.O. Box 2208, Carson City, NV 89702, 1-800-729-4131

ISBN: 1-893157-05-9

Cover design by The Right Type
Printed in the United States of America
10 9 8 7 6 5 4 3 2

The question of "who?" is the focusing energy of the "messages" is a difficult question to answer tactfully and yet completely. "Isness" is the focus to be sought by each individual awareness. As each expands within the process of self-identification so does the ability to allow the flow of "Isness" to move through their experience. Each will attract into their awareness knowledge to live into wisdom. The vibratory rate of the planetary environment and of the members of humanity on earth is low enough that this ability is currently virtually inaccessible. To assist willing members of mankind to access the necessary information to provide a way to transcend this current aberrant state, various volunteer awareness points within higher vibrational frequencies have acted as booster stations to focus this information through those willing to participate on the earth plane. Knowing the custom of earth's inhabitants requiring the "personify to identify" mode, names from the exotic to the ridiculous have been given as sources of this information. The information included exercises in discernment, most participants failed the discernment tests. Much was filled with profound truth, but much of it was drained of energy by the continual parade of victims wanting their personal problems solved for them. The information became distorted as the foci were withdrawn and the volunteers winged it (faked it) on their own for their sincerity was lost in the notoriety and greed that resulted.

In view of this history, it was the mutual agreement between the parties involved in the dictation/translation/transcription process for these messages that the identities of the foci involved would remain unidentified and there would be no monetary rewards whatsoever involved. Further, there would be no personal information disseminated for any one individual's benefit. The totality of the foci involved is for the benefit of the planet and its inhabitants, period! The truth of the messages is to be discerned and used for the benefit of humanity first and then gleaned by the individual to apply personally as part of the wholeness to which it is focused without the necessity of personal names to identify truth. If that is not understood, then the messages need to be read again to transcend this need into commitment to the holographic intention of the information they contain.

It is hoped that the succinctness of this message is accepted in the tone of importance in which it is intended. The window of opportunity to accomplish the necessary monumental consciousness transition is small compared to the obstacles within the human belief systems that must be literally dissolved so that the whole may be transformed.

It is sincerely hoped that the truth contained will be a sword that cuts through the armor of deception and lays open the hearts and minds of the necessary quotient for success.

II-1

There has been a great deal of interest in the independent activities of the people who have received and read the copies of the message and the handbook. As expected, the reactions have been mixed between total acceptance and total rejection. However, the overall impact has been gratifying and effective. There are indeed lights of understanding beginning to be discernable on many parts of the planet.

The assimilation and application of the concepts will accelerate the acceptance of the principles involved and through their application the desire for greater understanding will be increased. Therefore an opening will be created that will allow for movement toward the goal of a new paradigm and it will begin to manifest. When the time is ripe for greater expansion of the concept of a new experience for mankind, the information leading to the next step will be ready for distribution. Once the transition is made away from victim consciousness toward the acknowledgement of personal power through alignment with the originating expansive flow of creative energies, the thirst for greater understanding will be aroused. The misunderstanding of looking outward for answers is deeply ingrained and will require de-programming and education of how to apply this concept to daily living in order to allow it to become a new foundation for manifested reality.

Without adequate changes at deep levels of the psyche and application of the previous explained universal laws, the next levels of understanding will be nothing more than another exercise in entertainment. Much of the valuable information disseminated through other receivers has become an addiction for fanaticizing with little or no application in practical living experience. The focus has been toward survival of the physical body so that the same ideals and life style could be maintained until individuals could ascend (arise out of) rather than transcend (go beyond). The focus must be more wholistic and include survival for service aimed at lifting the yoke of darkness and descending vibratory experience from humanity and the planet rather than be focused on individual escape from the morass of a destructive situation. In other words, there must be participation in a solution rather than using the information to abandon the ship.

Once the goal is identified in a statement, then what comes next? What are the guidelines for participation that will ensure that transcendence through to experience the new paradigm? This will be the focus of the next level of information. Much material has been disseminated indicating that rescue and reform will be provided by extraterrestrial beings and all humanity has to do is to meditate and wait around for magical processes to change everything for them. It would be wise not to count on it. There is a saying. "God helps those that help themselves." That is a truth to put in a dozen places to remind you to let go of the "I am a victim that needs to be rescued" consciousness. **You will be helped but victims will not be rescued. Victim consciousness vibrates below the necessary levels to enter higher dimensions.**

Giving up victim consciousness is a personal decision. It is not an easy process. If you rescue, you become a victim of the rescued. Sympathizing with those who are locked into victim consciousness supports their victimhood and ties you to them. Discernment allows you to recognize the situation and at that point you must acknowledge that this is a situation that is of their own creation through their belief that others control their choices. This does not mean that you must ignore their plight, but does determine that you cannot do for them what they are unwilling to do for themselves. There is not a rule of thumb for how to give wise assistance to them. Their plight is a result of the personal decisions they have made and the attitudes that have influenced those decisions. Remember, they are human beings becoming or not, by their own choice. Teach them the prayer and remind them of it in the midst of their miniseries and tactfully suggest other viewpoints to them as you become aware of them. With the application of the "becoming" prayer, opportunities will abound for them.

The critical point for the next step in the transcendence process follows the acceptance of the personal ability to move through victim consciousness by accepting responsibility for using the universal laws to take charge of their manifested experience. This does not mean that each must become a millionaire to prove they have accomplished this. In truth most will find that abundance is measured by the inner feelings of self-approval and confidence that precludes the necessity of impressive material demonstrations for ego aggrandizement. What you do with regard to self and others is more important than what you have. When this is accomplished all that is necessary is attracted without effort, for each is then encompassed within the expansive flow of creation.

To become is the goal of all. How this is to be accomplished is uniquely experienced through freewill choice. Help is available. The asking must be for help not rescue or to piggyback on someone else's accomplishment. Each must know theirs is a unique experience not to be compared to others. Each incarnation is for their own particular soul purpose to be created through their choices and decisions. There are no mistakes other than to remain closed to seemingly new concepts and continue to repeat the current experience for lack of discernment of the connection to that which has focused each into manifestation. That connection vibrates within the awareness of every human and is ignored or responded to with each and every choice and decision. It is our goal to trigger the awareness of this connection in every human possible through direct connection or through changes in the mass conscious awareness on a planetary level, using what you refer to as the 100th monkey theory. First and foremost is transcendence of the victim consciousness into personal responsibility.

This process will require that individuals separate themselves from those refusing to change their perceptions and to align themselves with others who are willing to make this change. When lives begin to change as a result of accepting and using personal responsibility through the application of the universal laws, those previously unwilling to change will again choose to follow suit or not. Remember that freewill is the loose cannon of the 3rd dimension and the freedom to choose is made by *all* whether they admit it or not. Though it may seem that the victim/personal responsibility theme is being nauseatingly repeated, it is the foundation upon which the format for transcendence to the higher dimensions is built. It is the rock from which the foundation is quarried. It is the first step that begins the journey. Lip service is easy. It is in the doing that the proof of the pudding lies. How it is accomplished is between each person and the creative aspect that focused each into manifestation. Through the intuitive understandings that this connection fosters, each will find their purpose and the path of their journey. In the asking for help the opportunities that genuinely "feel" right will present themselves. Incorrect choices will be difficult and bring little satisfaction. Asking for discernment brings knowingness and other opportunities to pursue. A house will stand on a rock foundation and allow for layer upon layer of brick to be added. To begin, you must begin at the beginning.

II-2

The bible has a reference to two standing in a field, one is taken and the other is left behind. Does this support the belief that there will be an evacuation of part of humanity by space ships? In this case, the reference could be applied to a faith in the creative process and to coming into alignment with the expansive self-contemplative flow of energy that births each soul expression into manifested experience. When that alignment reaches a degree of compatibility that allows for a transition to higher dimensional experience, the transfer can be completed during the life experience. It "can" but it is a rare happening when the planetary whole is vibrating at the present rate. It has been a long time since that has taken place, contrary to some circulating stories. This is not to say that some blending experiences have not happened. Insofar as massive space ship removals of humans from this planet, as has been circulated, contemplate 6 billion plus beings and consider how many ships with facilities for them this would take and the answer is obvious. If humanity, experiencing as they are now, were transferred to another planet, there would be two planets in trouble instead of just one.

Each and every being on this planet came with the purpose of bringing the situation here into alignment with the cosmic plan of freewill experience leading to balance. That constitutes a lot of intention. That intention is there to be tapped in order to bring this situation to completion. When humanity, or at least a significant portion of it, can go *through* this situation and heal it themselves, then and only then can they move through their intention to come into balance. In the greater picture of each soul's evolvement, none would choose to be rescued. At the base of the rescue stories lies the victim consciousness. Does this render those messages false? That is for your discernment. Always there is truth to be found, and it is different for each. Ask the knowing part of self for discernment and proceed from that point to consider and you will know.

The presence of an energy cycle called the photon belt is circulating. It has been reported as being seen as a doughnut shaped energy field near the Pleiades star system. Does it really exist? Indeed, it does and calling it a cycle is the key to what it truly is. Regardless of what has been "seen", it is a transition of movement between the polar experiences of positive and negative, your terms. This experiencing has been pictured by many as a pendulum type movement from one extreme to the other. This would be appropriate in linear thought; however, higher dimensions are not experienced in a linear process. Since the great part of experience is in higher dimensional expression, the explanation must be thought of in holographic terms. Religious writings contain some references to wheels within wheels that indicate there are multiple cycles that are in motion and interfacing with each other. This brings to mind the workings of a mechanical watch. However, now you have watches that keep perfect time without those wheels. In this way, cycles can also be in process that are not necessarily circular in motion. Even though circular motion is observed going on around you, such as the motion of the solar system, and the zodiac, from the greater holographic prospective, these circular motions are spiral rather than circular, allowing for the expansiveness of the creative energies. If indeed, they were circular, then all that is would be static rather than expansive. This would limit evolvement and as you can easily contemplate, boredom and death would indeed be truth. From this perspective, you can now understand the importance of expansiveness as being at the basis of creation and how evolvement is a natural constituent of experience. With this as a frame of reference, you can begin to grasp that the spiral is accomplished by interlacing the polarities with the circular motion to widen the circle and to either lift or lower the continuity. The shift of energies that are necessary to accomplish the transition between the polarities is something like an electrical charge. It is accomplished by entry and passage through an energy field that causes a change in polarity. These energy fields are also in motion and move through the galaxy in cycles that coordinate with all other cycles with mathematical precision.

Planet earth is now poised at the transition point of several cycles. This is an occurrence that does not happen frequently and is of great interest to this portion of the galaxy. The result of these coinciding cycles is that the transition between polarities will be of greater impact and import enhanced by the fact that the consciousness of the beings and the planet poised to do this. These are not at the level of evolvement that was intended through the failure to make the transitions that were available in the last approximately 26,000-year cycle. Added to this, is the deliberate plan of the adversarial forces to disrupt the cycle transition into deliberate chaos intending to continue the negative polarity cycle for their own purposes. This then brings into understanding the necessity for the humans on this planet to make a leap in consciousness in order to survive this transition of energies into the next cycle by coming together in a mass consciousness that has a combined focus of an increased frequency. The upliftment through the release of victim consciousness into personal responsibility is the shift that would accomplish this necessary change. The degree of shift in the mass consciousness will determine the intensity of the planetary experience at a point within the energy field you call the photon belt and the ability of humanity to experience the transition through it.

It will also determine the ability of the adversarial plan to accomplish its purposes. Needless to say, their plan will never be allowed to be successful, but the question remains as to what part earth's inhabitants will play and where the soul awareness will find itself when the scenario plays out. It must be emphasized here that the ground crew is included in this drama, volunteering to help also carries with it the responsibility of becoming part of the destiny of the planetary consciousness. There will be no rescue. Each will rise or fall within that destiny. This then fuels the necessary commitment and focus of energy in helping humanity to accomplish this last ditch effort to come into vibratory alignment.

II-3

When the time comes for the changes to begin in earnest with regard to the change of governmental focus, there will be an outcry by the citizens. Measures are planned so that the individual will be overwhelmed and unable to react in any way but to submit. It is expected that they will grovel before the god that is on his throne far away and think that they are being punished for some great sin, in other words, play the victim. The inner strength of the focus of the soul has been totally disregarded. The planned shock of overwhelming the citizens as a whole has been analyzed and studied to bring forth the reaction that is desired. As in all experiments, the outcome is influenced by the expectations of those setting up the criteria. The "scientific" data so prized by the scientists of this era is as accurate as the opinions of the moment allow. Thus as new possibilities are considered, the old theories crumble eventually and are replaced. This indicates that the possibility exists that the expected reactions of humanity might indeed be replaced by *actions* that do not fit their planned scenario.

Mankind has been taught to distrust his fellow beings. Few have any realization of the interconnections that exist through the sharing of the source of their manifestation into experience. Since all are emanations of the creator focus in self-contemplation, you can rely on the fact that there are connections that are unknown and power within these connections that is wholly untapped. We have previously discussed the concerns of the situation as it presently exists on this planet and the importance of the convergence of the cycles with regard to the importance of the transitions that are available. It has been emphasized that all levels of consciousness including the creator are focusing upon this process. At this sequential place in the scenario, watchfulness is all that is being focused. However, when it is appropriate you may be assured that activation of latent abilities that are available within the consciousness and the physical structure of the human body can and will be stimulated.

The ability to receive this stimulation and accomplish what will be needed will depend upon the conscious awareness and in particular the ability to accept self-empowerment within a wholistic pattern of behavior. The energies that will be encountered in the approach to and passage into what you refer to as the photon belt will not be the same as are being experienced now. The last of the current polarity cycle is reaching its completion. Here again it is difficult to put into linear terms for your understanding processes that are of a holographic nature. Within a holographic framework, all is interactive within a cooperative format. When an imbalance is present all that remains in balance becomes focused to regain the balance of the whole. There is a generation of interactive energies to awaken latent connections to bring forth whatever is necessary to allow the return to balance. We return again to the understanding that thought has the capability to think. All that is manifest in all forms is thought into being from pure potentiality and is interactive within itself; this is a natural process. In its simplest explanation, each human is a thought that thinks and therefore is self-aware. As above, so it is below. The entire galaxy, and more, is thought that thinks and is self-aware.

The goal of the new paradigm in simple terms is the transition of humanity from victim consciousness into self-empowerment, which will result in a rise in the vibratory emanation of the planet and its inhabitants. Planting the means to make this transition is the goal of this segment of the ground team. Once planted and released to accomplish its intended effect, the stimulation of the latent connections will move it through the mass consciousness to all humans able to accept and begin to function within its concepts. The next step to follow will be the spread of the understanding of the four basic universal laws and the application of these within each individual experience. These concepts are included in the handbook and once the critical few begin to study and practice them, more latent connections will begin to open to the stimulation that will be coming to the planet with increasing frequency.

It is easy to get caught up in the fear of what might happen based on the present consciousness of the planetary inhabitants. However, it is important to stay within the understanding that this consciousness is ripe for change and that it is now underway. There are other ground teams accomplishing their assignments that dovetail and provide the holographic synthesis that is now taking shape. The situation is not hopeless, but is encouraging indeed! As each member has been stimulated into awakening to their assignments and have proceeded, most times through the need to do whether it made any logical sense or not, so also will that process spread through the mass consciousness. You have been programmed to distrust your humanness. Through empowering the personal self, it is necessary that you choose to trust the empowerment of your fellow man. Will there be exceptions? Yes, there will. One of the latent functions that will be stimulated will be discernment. You will know and when you trust the process, those will not be encountered. Victim consciousness will draw victim experience through the law of attraction. Those who move to self-empowerment in a holistic way will continue to evolve into greater experience and be drawn together to create the new paradigm.

This is not a message of deception. You are thought capable of thinking. There is a group consciousness that thinks. You can change your mind (thinking) and so can it. It is a matter of seeding the process with an alternative that has powerful appeal. Once put into usage its power increases, especially if it receives additional input from the concerned foci of greater levels of manifested awareness. Physical manifestation is an end result of focused thought. If through choice <u>and</u> request the focused thought is changed, then the physical manifestation must also change.

This understanding is easy to forget with the continued input of mind controlling data that is purposefully focused into daily experience. This is the reason each is encouraged to continue to reread and study the handbooks. The information is simple, direct and contains no techniques other than offering a solution that dovetails within the flow of expansive energies that maintain all creation and allow it to continue within the universal laws. The freewill aspect is both the thorn and the blossom of the process. It is the vital emanation of creative energy. It has at its essence both positive and negative polarity and is not bound by cycles. The polarities are available on the whim of decision which allows it to alter creation at the manifested level. Freewill cannot be controlled. It can be influenced, but at any point, individual consciousness can simply change its thinking and the influence is cast aside. Thought can create an experience and thought can change it into another experience entirely. Combined focus of thought is all-powerful when it operates within the universal laws and is supported by emotional commitment. The return to self-empowerment following the experience of containment and victim experiences will bring forth an emotional sensation to the soul that equates to the joy so often spoken of by religions. Just as love and hate cannot share the same heart, neither can joy and a victim perception share the same experience. The courage to choose comes as the responsibility of humanity to create its experience, in this instance with all possible help available for the asking.

II-4

There was a time in which the beings on this planet resided elsewhere in the galaxy. Not in the present body, but you would say these were your ancestors. Mankind did not originate on this planet. To those who currently believe that you came into being out of some primordial soup, this shall be an affront to that theory. However, through consideration of the laws of the universe, remember that creation is possible through intent and purpose. Development of body, mind, spirit and emotion does not fit into the criteria of random selection as a possible scenario. Indeed the physical body does match the physical attributes of the earth mineral content, but that is through the law of attraction that allows for adaptation within the environment. The marvel of the human body is that it has adaptive capabilities that make it possible to survive in hostile environments. This is surely being proven by the introduction of purposeful chemical abrasive combinations and vibrational variations designed to destroy it. The plan being that only the most adaptive will survive and be useful in further experimental adaptation and exploitation. Resistance to a negative environment allows for adaptation and can be stimulation to either advancement or regression, depending on the degree and the focus of the individual desire to move through the experience.

This possibility can now be discussed openly as the subject of extraterrestrial presence has been the subject of extensive media presentation. Though many older people still resist the possibility, most children accept it as true and dream of traveling to take part in other planetary experiences. Much of this is presented because of the belief that there is little left to be known about this planet and that adventure will soon be found only by exploring the space beyond. The popularity of the long-standing Star Trek series exemplifies this. The information as to the monumental number of solar systems that frequent this galaxy and the presence of numerous other galaxies that are being observed makes the possibility of other life supporting planets refute the assumption that this is the only planet with conscious life. Yet to be known is a way to construct and power appropriate craft to enable humans to traverse space. With the number of inhabitants draining the life force of this planet, the possibility seems beyond reach.

Indeed, humanity is at a crossroads of multiple levels of experience. How indeed are they going to come *through* this crisis?

Obviously not without help! In their arrogant stubbornness will they ask for it and accept it, if it is given? That can only answered as the situation progresses. As has been pointed out before, help cannot be given to those locked in victim consciousness. The solution lies in humanity creating its own solution and victims cannot accomplish this because of their desire to be rescued. Rescue demands that someone or something outside themselves accomplish whatever feat is required. Again the discussion returns to the same realization that a choice in how to experience manifested life faces the inhabitants of this planet. It is no longer survival of the fittest, but survival of the personally responsible.

The opposite experience of the victim is currently achieved as exercising power over other victims and has become an unending chain of interlocking experience for an incredibly long duration. That chain is long overdue to be broken. Its strength lies in the failure of those involved to choose another way of experiencing. Without the awareness and understanding of the universal laws that support successful evolving life experience, the chain remains unbroken. Humanity can change this longstanding experience, break the chain and return to the evolving citizenship of the galaxy/universe by choosing responsibility and applying the laws in their daily experience both individually and as a group. Because of the presence of polarity, when those are drawn together as a group this also repels those who choose otherwise, and a great division is made. The application of the laws creates a cooperative situation that allows for protection from the fear of the actions of the other groups in most surprising ways. The vibration increases rapidly and protective means are most creative indeed.

The question arises from a point of overview, if victim consciousness is present in our experience, then is it present within the consciousness of the creator? The obvious answer is yes. The creator is in self-contemplation for self-evolvement. At this level, the tiniest imbalance must be fully understood and cleared. You are that clearing process. When you move through it and arrive at personal responsibility, another phase of that imbalance is resolved. A wisely pruned vineyard produces a prolific healthy crop. Once this imbalance is pruned from your experience, yours will be a healthy and prolific experience!

It is not our purpose to assail the current beliefs in a frontal attack causing resistance and stress, but to give a gradual and convincing alternative to lives that have been lived in frustration and grim survival. Ending lives in pain and disease is demonstration of the soul consciousness of the denial of a solution by those experiencing this descending cycle of manifested circumstances. What appears as a complex and impossible situation has a simple solution. A change of attitude and application of simple understandable laws will provide the passageway through to new experience. Creation does not provide for suffering to buy anything but more suffering. It is a freewill choice. Therefore it is time to opt for a new experience by giving up what does not work and has not worked for an eon of sequential episodes.

The laws of attraction, intention and allowing used purposely through freewill choice are the criteria that will allow for the freedom of humanity and its return to full galactic citizenship and the ability to travel freely. Failure to follow these guidelines will require placement of those individuals into another learning situation. You are being offered the opportunity to begin again with the basics and incorporate them into your experience and surge ahead in a leap of consciousness that is unparalleled. How sad it will be if you stubbornly refuse to take advantage of the opportunity.

II-5

At the time of the greatest experience of chaos there will be moments of discouragement and wondering if any of this material was of value. It is then that each of the members of this ground team must hold fast to the understanding that change cannot and does not happen if the old structures remain in place. Therefore it is exactly through this chaos that the new paradigm of experience will come into being and it will not be long in manifesting. When the outline of it is held in place in the hearts and minds of the dedicated and committed humans that desire the replacement of the old with the adventure of the new, it will come quickly. There will be those who will falter, but with at least one of every cell group having the strength to hold tightly to the commitment, the cell will hold together and the focus will be held.

Many have questioned how that, in the meetings of the groups held worldwide, a single statement could arise from the many dream scenarios. Here we have the necessity of invoking the creator presence at each group interaction. In the creator self-contemplation process, each and all are known intimately. Inasmuch as at the point of inception of the entirety of the process there is one mind, one focus, then by invoking the focus that knows itself, one focus of truth is the inevitable outcome. Through this process an experience of the "oneness" that has been touted will indeed be experienced. Lip service has been given to this, but what it truly is has yet to be experienced in this dimension of consciousness. It has been described as "enlightenment, a feeling of being one with all." These few who have felt one with nature, etc., have not brought mankind one bit closer to each other. The creator wants his self-aware aspects to come into a *knowing through actual experience* of this greatest of all experiences. When a committed portion of humanity can come together in a single focus of purpose and truly commune with the creator energy, then oneness with each other will indeed be experienced and a leap in consciousness will follow and will enliven this project in ways beyond imagination.

As has been mentioned before, there is no reason that the creator cannot use every situation as a springboard for greater creation. When you contemplate the above scenario, knowing the ripple effect, can you imagine the experience of this leap in consciousness spreading through out creation and what effect it could have? Now you have a reason to believe that this is indeed an auspicious opportunity for mankind and one not to be missed! The issue of separation has been experienced through out this galaxy in a festering of negative actions between individuals, nations and planets long enough to be thoroughly contemplated and it is now time to resolve it and move beyond and into new adventures and opportunities.

This is a short discussion and one that needs careful and in depth consideration. Hold this information at the center of your personal commitment for your participation and focus. It is the reason that you made this decision to take the risk of being a member of the ground crew.

II-6

We are now ready to begin the adaptation of the human spirit to include a greater evolution and the pivotal turn to begin the return path to the creator than has been the current experience. These have been considered the experience of saints and most times simply not acknowledged or even known. Adaptations to the body have been made in the past within the genetics of the physical body itself and through the addition of vibratory implants. These have left a residue of effects that have in turn influenced the spiritual aspect. These changes have limited the vibrational connections to the focused source that has brought each into their physical expression. The genetic changes that were forcibly imposed on the human body were such that they have been inherently passed from one generation to the next and adaptation has not transcended all of these. Even the implants that caused great trauma have left their influence within the molecular memories of the cells and have been retained for generations. Modern man has been programmed to deny that humanity in its present physical form is very old indeed. It has indeed acquired some changes that do not serve it well at all.

From the larger aspect, the planet also suffers from similar changes that cripple its ability to function properly. It is time to bring these back into balance. Since it is apparent that neither the human body nor the planet are able to make these repairs in a fashion that is timely enough for the transitional opportunity, then help is necessary. In our previous discussions the process of thought manifesting into physical experience using the law of intentional focus explained that thought held with purposeful intention allows for manifestation. The intended thought through visualization of it in completion and vibratory stimulation of it through emotion, held firmly in place by commitment brings manifestation. Because the vibratory energies are at a low rate for manifested experience on this planet, the time necessary to manifest into form perceivable through 5 sensual experiences is slow indeed.

However, you are further reminded of the awareness of the planetary situation that is being observed by the galactic neighbors, most of whom are existing in a higher vibrational state of existence than planet earth. It is perfectly acceptable for the humans on this planet to invoke their help to manifest a change in the human body to accommodate the correction of the vibrational matrix of the human body and return it to its *intended pattern.* This request for help would require only a small number of human beings to enlist this help. It is something the ground crew could do inasmuch as they are now experiencing as 3rd dimensional human beings.

This would allow them to be the first to make the vibrational transition and to allow them to establish the ideal; the return of the archetype as it was originally created within the galactic equations. This then becomes the second major assignment of the ground crew. It is a simple statement within the positive prayer/mediations of each member remembering that this includes the grateful appreciation that this archetype already exists and is manifesting in perfection for each and *every* human body wherever it presently exists. It is important here to note that the archetype allows for evolution toward greater perfection of higher vibratory experience and this return to the archetype will not cause a problem for those who have achieved these changes.

This process allows for humanity to tap into the energies that are awaiting an opportunity to participate in resolving this situation and provides those assisting the greater opportunity to participate in the energy transition of the cyclical spiral of ascendance. Indeed, this provides the inclusion that is desired. Participation is by invitation only and you will be providing this opportunity. It is suggested that you contemplate the possibilities of this situation.

Reread this information as necessary in order to grasp the magnitude of this opportunity for all that are involved, including your pivotal role. Each can obviously realize that each is an extraordinary being with very specific commitments to complete as the sequence of divine order unfolds in personal experience and of the planet as a whole. The opportunity to "become" is ripe with promise in return for focused intention, purposeful follow through, and creational application of the suggestions contained within these communiqués.

II-7

As each of you became involved within this focus and began the process of composing your individual thoughts to contribute a possible statement of purpose, it became obvious to you that the simple statement required to appeal to all of mankind was not simple to arrive at. In the moment of this writing it has not yet come forth. The prayer of becoming is not yet widely known. This invocation can set the stage for opening the consciousness to perceive the statement when it is brought forth. The change in consciousness by those using the prayer with diligence in their daily life is interesting to observe. When it is further combined with a conscious clearing of accumulated negative attitudes and letting go of false doctrines from the awareness, it brings about clearly detectable vibrational increases observable by each individual. As the individual vibrations increase, the ability to connect with the source of each is enhanced. The connection itself begins to enliven and allow the body to receive a greater quantity of supportive energy. It is as though this flow of vital energy has been squeezed or pinched so that the flow is barely enough to maintain life. Contrary to what is taught, without this flow of energy from the source that focused each into being, life cannot be maintained in the body. At the center of each focus of awareness and within the physical body is a connecting point that receives this energy flow. When this flow of energy is broken or withdrawn, death occurs. The more intense the negative energies that are active in the body such as anger, fear, hate, etc., the less energy the body itself is able to receive of the already diminished flow. As these are intentionally released, the invocation of help "to become" re-activates the connection with each additional repetition.

You, the ground crew, are the guides in the setting up of the suggested procedures to uplift your fellow humans in the very near future. It is you that demonstrate the feasibility of these proposals and have input as to the viability of these reminders and suggestions. Reminders and suggestions are exactly what these messages contain. Since most humans now are lost within the complexity of their life experience amid the programmed onslaught of overwhelming control, it is obvious without help "being" let alone "becoming" is a lost cause. The numbers of inhabitants long ago became too overwhelming to consider removal as an option. This too has been planned for the universal laws for balanced life, including those regarding procreation, were deliberately convoluted and withheld. Warlike tendencies were over-stimulated from the natural instinctual self-defense/survival modes of behavior. The review of imbalance could go on and on, but that is not the point. The point is that a U-turn must be made by humanity in order to come through this experience, but the major portions of minds are programmed to reject the suggestions to do so.

Thus we must reach those that are open or desperate enough to grasp at whatever straw might possibly lead them to a different possibility. Each of you determines whom these people might be and are relied upon to make contact with them in an expansive outreach effect. Meanwhile the births continue and the control program also expands its influence and effects. Within this situation, these messages attempt to give as much help as possible to assist in remembering whom and what you are and to guide each in personal adaptation and evolvement to the greatest extent possible. All this is being done through a type of dictation/translation/transcription process that has its limitations.

Behind this seemingly vague yet ambitious process is the impetus of the creator focused energy. It has seemingly decided that the self-contemplation process of control, violence and victim/martyrdom has reached the point of resolution and transcendence. This awareness is now moving through the vibratory levels of awareness and those in the 3rd dimension are to get the message one way or another. Each of you is now a Rowan and has the message in hand. The question is, not can you, but will you deliver it?

II-8

Listening to the media reports of the situation in the "world at large" each is given the impression that ominous events portend the future and nothing of great danger is eminent at the center of "democracy's bastions." Only distant areas of ethnic unrest are subject to volatile situations of violence. These areas are chosen to exploit because there are few people to people connections between the people of the USA and people in those countries. Yet through military "assistance" the USA is involved to a far greater degree than any of the other members of the UN coalition. With your approval of these acts by default, the perceived image of the USA has been transformed in the eyes of the world from the home of the brave and free to that of the home of the dark avenger, satan. All this has taken place in a gradual transition that has been and continues to be purposely apparent in all areas of the world but in the USA. Those caught up in the aggression and those in the watching world assume that this transition has your full and complete approval. Understanding that communication as it now exists was birthed in the affluent USA, it is then assumed that surely its citizens are fully informed and therefore are the impetus of the transition into this aggressive mode. It is incomprehensible to those in the rest of the world that these citizens are as a whole unaware that the aggressive acts are anything but benevolent "help" for there is little if any frame of reference for what those in war torn areas are suffering.

Where are the stories of the military personnel that return home who could confirm this claim? Each sees but a small segment of the whole picture. Indoctrination and mind control within the military is far more sophisticated than is possible with the general public. After discharge from the military services and a period of time away from these practices many of those involved begin to disassociate from the mind control effects and find themselves mentally and emotionally unstable. Help, other than drugs, to sort out the indoctrinated "suggestions" from the actual experiences is unavailable through government agencies and many are unable to function in the civilian world. They are left with the choice to either rejoin the military or cope in what ever way they can. Few if any have the finances or are able to find outside psychiatric help that comprehends the basis of their dilemmas. The programming of your beloved children is carefully designed to fit the categories of the future roles they will play in these armed intrigues of aggression.

When we compare the overall understanding of this situation as a play, it is appropriate. Though it is presented as if there were unbalanced authors writing scenarios to be deliberately acted out, there is more truth involved than can be imagined! Presenting this information to you, it seems to come forth in a melodramatic tone and the immediate reaction is to refuse to consider that such massive delusion could be perpetrated on so many million people. Human nature is well known. Your reactions and beliefs are fully understood. Nothing has been left to chance in this well planned game of illusion for the purpose of delusion. The USA is the ideal vehicle for this particular transition of global role reversal in as much as there are no long-standing ethnic animosities as are present in other areas of the planet. The black/white/native American issues are the only exploitable issues and they are not of such duration to bring about the same reactions as the Moslem/Jewish/Christian situations that are now in growing conflagration in the European and eastern countries.

At the base of this entire picture is the very "human nature" that has been so well examined and studied. Humanity has been led to spend its energies in the experience and exploration of the environment outside themselves. It is only in recent years that the medical/scientific community has begun to consider the understanding of the human physical body with sophisticated instrumentation. Unfortunately it has not been for the understanding itself, but because of the influence of the dark perpetrators through the chemical companies for the purpose of gain through treating symptoms of degenerating human bodies. This is the result of an overall planned assault on the human body to coincide with the natural consequences of the effect of over-population. The research for the dark purposes will seldom if ever be revealed, however some of what is learned by dedicated medical researchers is being published. Genetic research is much maligned and there is reason to be skeptical of the motives involved in the manipulations that are now possible in the inherent DNA structures of the human body. Ethically focused research could indeed bring about changes that would release mankind from destructive patterns of behavior and of inherent pre-dispositions to health problems and disabilities.

However, in the present global situation none of this is going to work itself out in a time frame soon enough to assist in the present moment dilemma of humanity and planet Earth. Therefore, it appears that creating a new paradigm of human experience is the only available solution. Though reviewing the same situations periodically in this material seem unnecessary, it is included again for the purpose of review and reinforcing the commitment that each of you have made to this project. With the continual deluge of disinformation, mind control and governmental super-snooping capabilities, it seems even more redundant that so many can be so unaware or in such deep denial. Even the opposition is amazed at its success! Thus they are engaged in seeing just how much can be paraded before your eyes without your awareness being triggered. It is a phenomenal experience to observe this continue to progress.

It is the job of the ground team to accept the reality of what exists, then to look *through and beyond* the global situation, lay the foundation of the new paradigm and aid in birthing it into manifested reality. The universal laws function and are available to those of understanding and intent to use them to their full potential. Deliberate intentional application of the first three will result in the fourth – the balanced experience of the new paradigm.

II-9

The honor and glory of this planet, its past history and its future role as a nurturing home to evolving humanity hangs in the balance as its degradation continues unabated. As it and its inhabitants sicken from misuse and abuse through ignorance and arrogant purposeful destruction of its resources and its supportive atmosphere, the mass consciousness becomes psychologically unstable. The extremes of behavior become more evident not only through reported bazaar incidents, but within each individual life experience. Addictions and antisocial behavior within all organized structures becomes more prevalent. The family structure that is experienced without the universal laws as the ideal format within in which to base its purpose and focus fails to provide the necessary education for children to evolve into mature and functioning adults. Instead of each generation spiraling upward into evolving knowledge, experience and wisdom, humanity has remained stuck in a continuing circle of abuse, ignorance and physical and spiritual poverty. Those who amass material wealth find themselves poor in spirit and thus continue to search for the fulfillment of the void within that is the ignorance of the existence within and the use of the laws it would provide.

Once the recognition is made that this nebulous feeling of lack is indeed real and that it can be resolved, the search for the answer to the puzzle comes about naturally, however the search for a teacher of this wisdom goes unrewarded. Those that are found teach doctrines that continue the ignorance. The true teachings that are recorded in ancient documents remain hidden, either yet to be discovered or have been found and deliberately withheld from dissemination to the people or destroyed. Little has changed over the centuries, for those who would control continue to keep the people in spiritual ignorance and poverty.

Thus the time is now ripe for the call of the people for release from this incessant control and denigration of humanity's search of its rightful path of evolvement. The focus of creation in this portion of All That Is has decreed that this must end. Mankind must stand forth in the truth of who and what he is and end this chapter in its history. In the millenniums of experience, it has not happened through their own doing. He/she remains stuck in such silliness as whether the information contains references that are "chauvinistic" and fails to extract the truth, for such things are of no importance. Man and (wo)man meaning mankind with and without a womb is one and the same. He is the same with or without the (s)he. Each is one with the creative energy that focuses them into existence and holds them there in the energy of love without excuses or judgment. Just as the creator has no greater love of one creature than another, all are held in the highest of esteem, all are then expected to do *likewise* (in wisdom).

The love of the creator and of the energy of creation is not the superficial romantic love of your songs and stories, but one of absolute support. If it were not so, it would be withdrawn at the least excuse and your experiences would be short indeed. A parent that fails to guide and reasonably and logically discipline a child lacks real love for that child. Few of the millions of children of this time on the planet are truly loved! They are tolerated, used, abused and forced to grow physically, but not raised up in the knowledge and understanding of who and what they are and what is expected of them in either the physical or spiritual realms of their life experience. At the bottom of this lies the indisputable fact that parents cannot provide what they do not themselves know. Most now refuse to pass on what was taught them for it has not led them to fulfillment; thus they send their children into adulthood with even less than they received.

None of the above does more than delineate the problem and does not provide a solution. The religions of the world offer up their "wise" writings as the answer, but these have been so adulterated as to provide only more circuitous searching. Thus it would appear that it is time that true guidance appear on the scene. The question then arises as to how this would or could be disseminated. Those in desperation that pursue the false religious doctrines are radical and fanatic in their defense and are no different than when the last great teachers walked among you. They are not less malleable in the belief that their priests and preachers are wise in their judgments and would again follow them into smothering any teacher or teachings that might be sent. How then could such enlightenment proceed? If indeed the real teachers, called Jesus or Mohammed, returned to walk and teach among their people they would be no better received, as their true teachings would be unrecognizable because these were altered and adulterated almost immediately. Even if they were allowed to teach, would these "new" and different teachings be received any more than the last time? They were heard, but the people could not accept them and apply them to their daily life and that is the proof of any pudding.

If mankind, male and female is to transcend this seemingly endless chasing of its tail through generations of suffering, then it must stop creating victims and being victims. It must grasp and understand that its purpose is the veneration, education and development of the awareness of its connection to its source, the tiny computer chip, the segment of creation itself that is their *self awareness!* The *I AM that I AM* awareness that is who and what each and every human being is, whether male or female, black, white, red, yellow or brown, earthling or alien. This awareness comes into "beingness" and through recurring experience quickly or slowly learns what it is taught, but not how to return from whence it came fulfilled. It is influenced totally by the parenting it receives through out its numerous experiences not only by others, but most importantly of all by itself. It accepts or rejects its opportunities to harmonize with its source and to extend that expansive energy into its choices of experience through attitudes and decisions.

It is not a simplistic process and thus cycles of experience are supplied over long periods to provide this process. To grasp the understanding that each is an individual extension of wholeness, likened to a cell within a body, in which all are individual yet part of a focused wholeness within a greater wholeness is an imperative. Just as within the human body, if cells attack and destroy the essential organs, the body cannot survive. Humanity must understand that it can no longer continue to destroy its own without destroying the wholeness that contains it. It must stop destroying the planet that nurtures it as well as each other. Repeating the same destructive patterns without transcending them is causing the sustaining planet, solar system and galaxy disease, imbalance and disharmony. The creator focus of this galaxy has the choice of helping this happen for all that are willing to accept this help and putting all those who purposefully refuse in a holding space so that the cooperative are no longer held back by the uncooperative. It is as simple as that and mankind is *now* facing this choice.

Teachers will not be put in a position to again become martyred victims for the purposes of those who are addicted to control and exploitation of their fellow humans. This will be a grass roots movement and will spread among the willing people who will grasp the understanding of who and what they are and change their consciousness accordingly. These will then spread the understanding among themselves and become their own teachers. The messages will be short and simple and each will apply them in their own way or not. Each will assume responsibility and will spread the teaching to all that are willing to accept and *allow* those who choose otherwise to go their own way. The time of self-awareness and personal responsibility that will allow the transcendence of this hopeless situation into a new paradigm of experience is now or the holding space is prepared and awaiting. It is opportunity or threat as your attitude determines.

II-10

At the center of your experience is the awareness that you are, that you exist. This awareness is separate and apart from your body and your brain. It can be likened to a tiny computer chip that continues to be programmed by what is experienced by you through your every thought, word and deed. Your observer ego writes the code and you act and react in accordance with that programming. The chip undergoes constant reprogramming as you add, subtract and change your thoughts, words, actions, attitudes and beliefs. To continue the comparison in computer terminology, the active memory is stored within the brain and the stored memory within the cells of the body and magnetic field that surrounds the body. The body itself can be likened to an alkaline battery. Thus when its overall pH balance is too acidic it does not function at its ideal capacity.

Your tiny computer chip is your personal connective portion of Creation with a capital, that which is All That Is, pure potentiality in contemplation of itself. You indeed are gods in training. Through your freewill you are allowed to figure out how to become a god, and the recognition of this begins your ascent toward or away from that goal. To desire to accomplish this ascent toward godliness is programmed within that chip and *cannot* be changed or removed. It remains no matter how much it is ignored or how many times it is overridden with other programming. It is always there waiting to be activated.

Inasmuch as you can know that you are, that you can observe that you think, act, make decisions, observe and experience with the 5 senses and more, is called self-awareness. It is that portion that is beyond the physical brain function. It is your bit of immortality. Now it is your opportunity to begin to increase your operating system through recognizing and honoring this chip thus utilizing its potential from bytes to bits, kilobytes, megabytes and gigabytes. The comparison of a human to a computer is more apropos than you can imagine. Indeed, computers are modeled from the human example.

Mankind without understanding that its root meaning from antiquity is "god-man" tosses about the word human. Where is this tiny chip that supposedly is at the center of the human experience? When the human is dissected, where is this marvelous chip? The answer is, can you see your awareness? The chip is the "Life force", the breath that is present at birth and leaves at death. It is the unknowable secret that we can only wonder if Creation knows. Is it the mystery that propels Creation to contemplate itself and because of that is it the reason that we exist and pursue the same contemplative experience?

II-11

In these messages, references to mankind and humanity are one and the same, with no deference or difference intended for male or female. He and his are intended as he/she and her/his entirely as equals, which they are, with properties of form and purpose that are unique and common. There are certain indisputable facts that are laid as groundwork for the story of humanity as it exists on this planet to unfold in a concise and understandable sequence.

- There are many inhabited planets in this and other solar systems.
- Many contain self-aware, intelligent life forms.
- Many are far-advanced in conscious awareness of who and what they are within Creation as it now exists.
- Interplanetary travel does now and has existed for what you would term as eons of time.
- This planet has been and continues to be visited.
- There are different purposes for these visits by different representatives from various planets.
- These visitors have and do interact at various levels with life forms on this planet.
- There indeed are benevolent beings of higher understandings that have been and are now committed to helping humanity on earth to cope with and transcend the future that is coming forth now.
- Within this understanding, what follows is a brief history of many thousands of years for this branch of the human family tree.

There was a time in which mankind was indeed a carefree being. What you would refer to as childlike. Just as your children begin life as dependent babes that progress through stages of playing life in their own reality despite the world of adulthood going on all about them, mankind was this kind of being, open, naïve, playful and easily influenced.

As explained before, creation is experienced within both the positive and the negative polarities, in a balance of travels to and from the point of equilibrium between the two. This can involve experiences of what might be termed aggression and acquiescence. Built into the focused awareness of all conscious (self-aware) life forms, is a balance for this experience of both polarities. You call it "self-defense", or the innate reaction of "fight or flight," triggered by the automatic insertion of adrenaline into the body. There was a group that through what you call genetic engineering changed their life form to eliminate this function. This allowed them to remain in the positive consciousness experience, a very pleasant way to live indeed. However, it left them defenseless in so far as any form of aggression was concerned. Their solution, instead of reestablishing this balancing function, was to find a less evolved species and have them provide this needed service for them. You guessed it! A group of less evolved humanoids. However, just to make sure they did their job, they were genetically engineered to enhance the adrenal output to make sure they reacted more aggressively than was natural. Too make a long story short, this change caused an imbalance that changed the personality and limited the ability of this altered species to know their innate connection to creation. Those who engineered this change then found their intended helpers unstable and threatening rather than being the protectors they had desired. The solution to their problem did not include reengineering the altered humans so that succeeding generations would return to normal since that failed to provide an immediate solution to their perceived problem. Instead they simply shipped them off to a sparsely inhabited planet in a far off corner of the galaxy where they were not likely be discovered, and blame for this failed experiment would not likely be placed on them, even if the forcibly mutated future generations were discovered. To ensure this, all memory of this experience was erased and no records were allowed to be taken by the altered humans on the trip to earth. In other words this branch of humanity was shipped off to what might be termed a prison planet and left to either destroy each other or perhaps eventually work out their genetic imbalance through adaptation. Impossible? Think back to the colonization of the USA or that of Australia. The nation of England emptied their prisons in that process, doing exactly the same thing with hopes of the same result.

Did this act of enslavement interfere with the freewill of this segment of humanity? Indeed it did. Why then was it allowed to proceed? The offending planet made the acts by their freewill choice, but through the law of attraction, so was the result of drawing to them a complimentary experience. The law of attraction works and cannot be escaped by ignoring fact and hiding the evidence.

Once you accept this premise, you begin to understand the situation that now surrounds you. However, there is more to this story. This trans-galactic shipment was not unobserved. Other advanced humans were aware of the scenario and have over the eons of time visited you. It became obvious that adaptation was not eliminating the genetic alteration. Thus a further experiment was begun. Your bible refers to visitors finding the daughters of men fair and mating with them. This was in hopes that the introduction of another gene pool into abandoned humanity would in subsequent generations eventually overcome the genetic alteration. If not, then the increased intelligence through the hybridization process might allow them to overcome the alteration through coming up with their own solution to the problem. From time to time the introduction of extra gene pool additions have been made through carefully chosen genetic matching. Progress has been made. However, the overwhelming result has been that the additional intelligence enhanced the aggressive tendency in many of the humans with the end result that aggressive tendencies within those not positively affected by the gene pool changes were reinforced with greater abilities to develop incredible applications of weaponry. They used the additional intelligence to organize to a high degree with the purpose of creating a hierarchy of power and control over the members of humanity on this planet that have evolved to a balanced genetic structure. Both of these negative results continue now.

This raises the question of whether the gene pool additions resulted in interfering with the planet in violation of universal law with regard to freewill. None of this was done without it being cleared through ruling councils of galactic beings that focus creative energy and oversee the balance of the galaxy. If you are focused thought thinking, which you are, then there are levels of focused thought thinking greater thoughts than you can yet imagine. There are benevolent beings that are part of the plan of creation that entails responsibilities of overseeing the galactic maintenance and expansion process. Because genetic development was approved for this planet, other visitors have come to this planet as a source of gene pool improvement for their planetary inhabitants. This has been carried out with carefully selected individuals. Approval for this is given by these individuals before hand through a process that will purposely not be discussed at this time.

There is much knowledge that you have been denied that it is your right to know. Through manipulations by those still caught in the throws of the genetic alteration that require them to pursue control to support their violent tendencies, you have been denied this information, even though it has been brought to earth many times. The benevolent beings have walked among you teaching, and because of being attacked and killed, have then come undetected to continue the gene pool experiments with selected recipients, educating them through clandestine meetings in attempts to bring you into the awareness of who and what you are.

Unfortunately, the powerful controllers distort the teachings and use them for their own gain and you are left bereft of the needed knowledge to lift yourselves from this morass of violent behavior.

The happy news of this story is that there are sufficient numbers of genetically different humans now residing on this planet to change the behavior pattern of the planet back to the normal range. They must, however, find out whom they are and what to do. The question that remained for the benevolent ones, was how to do this. If they came themselves, the weaponry would be employed and death would be the end result. The teachers they instructed have ended up with the same result and the teachings altered to suit the purposes of the aggressive ones. How then are the wheels to be set into motion to bring this situation to an end?

Telepathic, mind to mind communication, is a common attribute of humanity, but was lost to the humans marooned on this planet in the genetic alteration. Through the gene pool change a significant number of earth's inhabitants had this ability come into being quite naturally in a rudimentary form. Those benevolent beings that use telepathic abilities as a normal part of life found they could communicate with many of the genetically enhanced beings in recent generations. However, this was as successful as the knowledge and understanding of the earth human allowed since the knowledge imparted had to be filtered through their understandings and vocabulary. Total awareness of the earth human could also be pushed aside with the human's permission and the higher awareness could speak directly, however this process was limited by the benevolent beings understanding and awareness of what the human experience entailed. Because of this lack of understanding at each side of the process it was difficult for humanity to understand the teachings or to accept the process at all. This process has been known as channeling. Partial teaching has been accomplished, but it has not been entirely satisfactory. However, no better way to communicate directly has yet been devised. The enhancement of the understanding of the receiving human has been the only solution thus far so that more clarity can be incorporated into the information.

In order that what is understood from the information made available thus far reaches as many of the genetically corrected humans as possible, it was necessary that the information be spread without being distorted by the controlling powers. Thus the enhancement in information speed and various means of it were allowed to be given, even though it was assumed that the aggressive group would use it for their own purposes. However, at this time information to the genetically normal humans can travel to them quite freely. The problem of the moment is to get the information circulating.

It should be further noted that the information given through telepathic use of humans must be considered with the discernment of logic accompanied by the open mind of whether it could possibly contain truth. Truth is individually discerned through the screen of life experience and should be weighed and considered carefully by each person. Enhanced communication is also in the form of books that now contain careful research of what you would call ancient history. These bring forth information from the time in which the benevolent beings from other planetary systems could walk on the earth in safety. These visits were recorded in the language and art of the day. Lacking photographs and written word understood by many people, myths were told by words and simple symbols that have been misinterpreted both innocently and purposefully. The enlightened teachers purposefully hid much information for later discovery. Some has been found in recent times and has been either destroyed or hidden from you soon after the discoveries. News of more accurate decoding of what is available is becoming commonly known and is available in books. These books must be read with a great deal of discernment as often-erroneous assumptions were made as to the meanings of the decoded information. It is much more difficult for it to be concealed or misinterpreted because of the education levels of much of humanity and the freedom with which information can now flow between people. It is hoped that many will search out the information and in a continuing effort attempt to interpret the information. It is necessary that they come into an understanding that allows them to realize that this is a momentous time for those who are now capable of changing the destiny that is planned for them by the organized aggressive fellow humans on this planet.

II-12

The momentous time for humanity to transcend this seemingly unsolvable dilemma is repeated with purposeful intent. The profusion of communication modes and content is overwhelming and is designed to direct mankind away from physical activity and into an imbalance of mental activity. This promotion of a sedentary life style weakens the physical body, prevents the release of stress and lessens the likelihood of survival in the days ahead. In order to transcend the experience of this repetition of life as guided by others, and to replace it with a life of personal responsibility, each must be present in a body on this planet. The opportunity to do this is here now, but your availability to participate is based on your personal internal choice. The word internal is chosen specifically, for how you come to know who and what you are is a process of internalizing within your own awareness and pondering these different ideas. There must be consideration of them in focused thought and definite decisions reached that are meaningful and followed by active changes in each life focus. These processes are best carried out in quiet time alone. In order to do this within an experiencing mode of work, family and social commitments that seem to leave little breathing room will require a decision to participate or not. If the decision is to participate, then your priorities of life will need to be changed. The TV will need to be turned off. The word "no" may need to be introduced regularly into your conversation. A great deal of contemplation can be accomplished on a solitary walk.

It must be understood that this discussion stresses a *personal* decision. Each must decide for him/herself. It is suggested that discussions with your spouse be encouraged, if that is appropriate. Many times ones in relationships have entirely different views in these areas. The pivotal relationship between you and your connection to creation is personal and can only be dealt with alone. To share with another person who is as committed to strengthening this connection is a joy. Through deliberate intention, those living on this planet include millions and millions that have been taught since early childhood to seek a greater connection to a "god" who is somewhere out there in the unknown. And that one can live a life of ease and luxury after death in some other mythical Utopian realm is illogical to visitors from spiritually advanced planets. This christian myth is paralleled by more beliefs almost as illogical in other religions.

Each child is first to learn the gift of self-awareness is the only god necessary for each to know. Then all of their life is experienced through this focus point with further learning that personal responsibility empowers it through their life experiences into either a positive or a negative perspective. At the maturity of a generation of this understanding, religion as it exists would become a moot point. Through the understanding that the amazing gift of self-aware experience is in all things supported by the simples laws of attraction, focused intent and allowance of freewill choices, and supported by understanding gained through experience using these basically simple truths, then a new experience would await them than exists now. This is an over simplification for the teaching would involve much guidance of these children. The question remains how could something that is not known by the parent be taught by them? Thus simply the knowing of the truth does not solve the challenges that present themselves. Each must begin at the point at which truth is discovered.

In the quiet of their own consciousness, individuals must stand above the situation, consider carefully the extent of the commitment each is willing to make and then set about incorporating changes through these new understandings. As each dilemma presents itself, the simple prayer of "I am a human becoming, help me to become, or we are humans becoming, help us to become, or they are humans becoming, help them to become" changes the internal climate and incorporates the difficult law of allowance into reality. The release of the need to control through allowance changes the perception profoundly. It allows transcendence from responsibility for others and recognizes the personal choice of releasing them to their own personal decisions. Rather than bringing forth feelings of separation, this blessing process brings forth an experience of a form of love that has blessed them in a way that will have profound effects on their life. In adversarial situations, a change may take several repetitions, but it will bring change.

What is being experienced within this opportunity is that

which is extended to each on a continuing basis by the point of harmonious thought within creation that focuses each individual into existence in the first place. If this were not the case, then with the first act contrary to universal law, the energy that holds each in manifested reality would be withdrawn and each would cease to exist. Each would be denied the experience of the result of that choice and could not then come into the wisdom of understanding that the act brought forth a result and provided the choice of repeating it or transcending it through wisdom. What exists within creation in truth is not religion as a practiced dogma, but practical, applicable, logical spirituality. Spirit being the name given to the presence of creation which is omnipresent, omniscient and omnipotent. In other words, the destiny of learning this truth and the experience of choosing to come into understanding and practicing it cannot be avoided, it can only be postponed.

Simplistic as this discussion is, it contains the basis for seemingly magical transformation in the life of those willing to adopt such change. To give up the known and travel into the unknown has long been the elixir of adventure. Mankind need not travel elsewhere from where he is or what he is doing to have adventure. All life is experienced by the attitude that is reflected within its own thoughts. What seems boring and mundane could be experienced differently by changing the parameters of experience, one situation at a time. As pressing as the situation is with regard to those who would enslave their fellow beings on a global scale, it can only be changed through individuals transcending their own belief structure.

It must begin with the recognition and realization that a longstanding series of deceptions, manipulations and misuses have been perpetrated. That this is true does not change anything.

Where mankind is now is where he is and thus blame, fear, over reaction or cowardice will resolve nothing. Resistance or the choice to retaliate will count for nothing. Two wrongs will never equate to right. It remains for mankind to swallow the truth and to look to his focused source and chose to change his experience by coming into the knowledge, understanding and application of the laws that support all of creation. God as known to humanity on this planet does not exist. He isn't dead because he never existed. Creation exists and has all the attributes of omnipotence (all power), omniscience (all knowing) and omnipresence. The only worship required is the living of the gift of self-aware life within the laws that have brought each into the experience with honor and appreciation for the wondrous privilege that it is.

Help to bring about the incorporation of this awaits invitation by humanity. Teachers in the form of benevolent beings will come again to walk among you on this planet when it is safe *and they are invited.* They will not teach you how they think you should live, but will teach you the laws of the universe and advise you in their application to the parameters of the life design you choose individually and as a group. The choice is here to be made now between slavery and difficult deaths or freedom to come into harmony with the way creation is meant to be experienced.

II-13

When the time arrives that the imposition of the final phases of the lock down of personal freedoms begins in earnest there will be resistance. Especially in the USA since of all the humans on the planet, they have been the most deceived, the most pampered and the most used. Difficult as it is for its citizens to believe, their national development has been guided and controlled from the very beginning. The natural ingenuity and creativity have been encouraged and then turned to advantage or "bought out" and shelved. A particularly appropriate example is the continued development of sources of energy and transportation that would end the dependence on oil and coal which would eliminate the health endangering of both the human body and the planetary flora and fauna. These are available to be developed very quickly in the context of the new paradigm.

There is a natural flow of expression that is part of the creative plan. It is what you might call unchangeable programming within the human pattern that remains regardless of what purposeful effort is made to override it. Once a goal or objective is decided upon by a personal choice that seems logical and accompanied by a commitment to that goal, it can and is pursued with all possible intensity, even to the point of giving up the life force to death. Methods of torture can and will cause the person to deny and pretend to give it up, but instead it usually instills it deeper into determination to resume the pursuit of its completion at the first opportunity. This is true for those goals that are both positive and negative in their energy configuration. Thus confrontational situations are the logical result. The positive impetus is pursued through logic and the negative experience through inability to apply the law of allowance and control becomes an addictive factor in the imbalance. It is important to comprehend that perfection is the ability to remain in balance in the practice of all the laws of the universe that support the expansive expression of creation. This is a process that gives challenge to participation within what is called eternity. If not for this monumental challenge, eternity could be boring indeed.

Intelligence is not confined to the human brain/mind. It is part and parcel of the potentiality that flows through the process of creation. Self contemplation by any manifested self-aware portion of creation, humanity for example, with a basic understanding of who and what they are in correlation to the expansive flow of creation, can transcend and remove limiting understandings. This then opens the awareness to the potential of new understandings changing the experience of that being entirely. In every way all experience serves the expansive process of each. Because creation is, at its potential, intelligence in pursuit of understanding itself, it is necessary to discern that all beliefs reach a point of limiting the opportunity to evolve. It is then a perpetual process of transcending and leaving behind each and every understanding into greater wisdom. The exception to this is the immutable universal laws that support the process as a whole. At the basis of these changes is always greater understanding of these laws, their utilization and the wisdom gained through the resulting experiences.

Certainly it would seem logical to the inhabitants of this planet that the time has come to transcend the present experience and change the beliefs that have focused creation into the experience of the future as it sits before them. It is far easier to perceive the situation at hand and change the beliefs to transcend the experience before it comes into complete manifestation. The negative polarity experience is brought about by failure to know, understand and apply the laws of the universe. You were set upon this planet without them and denied the knowledge of them. Those indigenous groups who were on the planet were learning them through observation of nature. Through the blessing of eternity, all the time necessary, their evolvement was on its way. Now, even these too have been corrupted. Unfortunately through the teaching of the theme that nature is to be subdued, rather than to be your teacher, you were denied the knowledge that could have been gained through its contemplation as a holographic example of the laws in application.

Is this saying that technology should be abandoned entirely and 6 billion people should return to indigenous living? That certainly would return the planet to 500 million people quickly through starvation. If living in that way would allow understanding of the universal laws, then it would be a worthwhile experience. However, knowledge of the laws from those who have both advanced technology and understanding is available to help, consequently the indigenous alternative would not be necessary. If mankind does not take responsibility to change the present intended scenario and the planet itself is required to change this situation, then technology will be purged and if the planet is "lucky" indigenous populations will again have the opportunity to evolve.

The consequences of ignoring this new opportunity to change the story of this branch of humanity that has been literally railroaded on to a path thousands of years long which has stymied their evolvement are not pleasant to contemplate. The scenario began through breaking the law of allowance and interfering with the evolvement of other humans and requiring them to remain stuck in "being" rather than becoming. The consequences to those through the law of attraction (what you give is what you get) was left for it to work in its inevitable way. No other group was willing to interfere accept in a benevolent advisory capacity, which is all that is allowed within the intelligent application of the universal laws. Intervention between species and planets does happen and is admitted here. However, the law of attraction absolutely works, but within the flow of divine order, the timing is left to the natural flow of that law within the intelligence of creation. To stretch the law of allowance and interact beyond the advisory capacity is carefully done with much consideration with regard to far reaching possible effects. This may be extended particularly when a group is evolved enough to ask for help specifically. The outcry to creation itself, by enough of the population, is answered by offers to help by specific groups. However, if the asking group is so closed as to be unable to recognize the offers, then nothing can be done. In this case, the outcries for help have been of such duration, and the imbalance of the purposeful negative perpetrators is so great, the whole galaxy is now focused on this small planet and orders have been issued to "find a way to answer the outcries." Thus earth's population is being presented with the current process and the current messages within the presently available communication proliferation. It is our prayer that it will be enough and in time.

II-14

Knowledge is given to mankind within the recorded history of the past that there has been communication with beings from other planets within the galaxy. The understanding that spiritual evolvement goes hand in hand with physical, emotional and mental evolvement would seem to be a logical assumption. Just as personal responsibility develops at the beginning levels through interaction with other beings, so also it continues as the path of evolvement unfolds through experience. Therefore, self-awareness involves itself through choice at greater and greater levels of personal responsibility interacting with other beings through maintenance of balance of physical creation, meaning the manifested galaxy as a whole. This is accomplished by sharing the responsibilities in cooperation. In other words, there is an organized administrative process in which to become involved as self-awareness and the ability to experience within the universal laws is attained in wisdom through experience. The benevolent beings that have visited your planet and now are indeed present in nearness to this planet are representatives who have volunteered for their own advancement to be part of this administrative focus of galactic maintenance.

In order for the expansive energy of creation to continue its outward flow, the individual points of self-awareness must continue within that flow through personal growth. Each must first recognize who and what they are and then through free will choose when and how to accomplish this within the laws of the universe. The desire to do this is literally programmed into each and every one and continues to call for fulfillment no matter how frustrated and blocked the experience or experiences are. Humanity on this planet is blocked at every turn by denial of this essential knowledge. The knowledge purposefully given has been distorted and the false idea that man is to use nature rather than cooperate with it so the example of it could be their teacher. Nature exists in harmony with the laws of the universe when left to itself and despite man's intervention and perversion of it. Nature keeps on trying because it contains the same element of programmed push to exist and evolve that is universal within creation.

The urge for expansive behavior is present within the living aspect of all creation. Only the self-aware have the privilege of freewill. That aspect of privilege contains the pitfall for exploitation of lesser expressions of creation. The inhabitants of this planet have created luxury and poverty through the use and abuse of the natural resources of this singularly beautiful planet. Distortion and ignorance, whether chosen or thrust upon intelligent beings, brings havoc and imbalance in ever widening effects. The personal choice to accept responsibility to change this carries the hope of this branch of humanity to transcend all of this while there is yet opportunity. Turning away from this opportunity will carry with it the consequences that naturally accompany it through the law of attraction. Eternity, as this cosmic cycle is called, is a very long sequential time in your counting to learn lessons ignored and refused. All help possible and beyond the normal process is being given now. The opportunity to literally leap ahead and bridge the lost chances of advancement is available for the taking. It is hoped that as many as possible can and will answer the call.

What are called crop circles have caused great curiosity. The previous discussion of the existence of the galactic administration of responsible maintenance was introduced as a preface for this information. In times of great stress for a planet, not an unusual thing in keeping all within balanced orbits, etc., energy is focused into the various grid systems that maintain orbit and spin velocities and other physical maintenance. It is similar to tuning up your automobile engine to keep it running at peak efficiency. This is done on a regular basis. In the case of your planet, which is under great stress, as even the most sleeping human will acknowledge, this process is going on with increased regularity. The crop circles are dynamic energy codes that are being sent as usual, but are being made visible as an attempt to awaken humanity to the truth that outside help is maintaining the balance. There have been specific cases of groups sitting in open fields, meditating and finding a crop circle created around them in moments. These instances were again for the purpose giving the message and took place only within the confines of these special areas and the particular timing of these transmissions and were not caused by the meditating group. The shapes vary with the specific energy patterns being focused. There are certain particularly restorative (for lack of a better word) areas that bring forth specific planetary responses. These shapes and places are matched for the response needed. These are not meant to be decoded, but rather to be accepted for their intended purpose.

There is knowledge and understanding of the galaxy and its encompassing universal laws available. It has always been available to be known. It is humanity's right to know all of it. That is known as evolvement. This grand opportunity is available for the simple taking of these messages, grasping the truth of the seriousness of the situation and acknowledging that lies and distortions have been perpetrated. Then learning and applying a few simple practical changes in perception through the application of the life energy that is who and what your are can begin. The choice is available now.

II-15

When the time comes in your awareness of sequential events, remembering that divine order does not operate necessarily in that mode, various situations will appear to have no connection at all to the intended purpose of thwarting the movement of the intended plan. Remember again how a computer graphic completes itself sometimes in linear movement and then the pattern changes in how it continues to appear. It must also be understood that the format of creation is not flat, but is *holographic and dimensional.* It is important to understand that those are not intended to be analogous. Manifested creation is holographic in form and dimensional in the context of vibratory variation. In other words, which are woefully inadequate to fully explain, a holographic form can exist in similar but different dimensional variations.

Once the inhabitants of earth accept the truth of the existence of other fellow inhabitants within this galaxy and others, the next great leap of understanding is that within their own galaxy there exists even more variation because each form can have dimensional variations. Further evolvement by way of knowledge and wisdom through applying the knowledge, it is possible to travel between the dimensions as easily as walking through a doorway. In other words a holographic form can exist in similar but different dimensional variations.

When this is understood, then traveling through space becomes comprehensible and does not seem at all impossible. It further explains how people of old regarded past interplanetary visitors as "gods" to be venerated and held in awe, resulting in religious worship. As understood then and perpetuated now by manipulating governmental and "religious" leaders, indeed the "god thing" is a hoax. Creational energies governed by universal laws through their application and the potentiality that underpins it is worthy of veneration, honor and awe, but there is no personality to receive worship. There is, however, that intangible, knowable bit of creational energy that is the self-awareness often called "heart feeling" with in you. That is worthy of veneration. It is there to be acknowledged and the power within understanding it used.

There are beings, that have come through experience to a greater and greater understanding of creation by conceptualizing and applying the laws that allow the use of this marvelous creational energy, that do deserve *respect.* Through their teaching, much can be learned by willing individuals rather than having to spend eons of time learning through trial and error. The greatest of all errors is to worship the teacher or the process rather than venerate the source and participate by acquiring knowledge and wisdom through experience. When mankind on this planet learns the truth of these words, then indeed he shall be free to continue his/her evolvement in 7 league boot strides. "I am a human becoming, help me to become" opens the door for the truth to be accepted. Each must forge their own path through their freewill choices, their attitudes, decisions and acceptance of their personal responsibility to participate in bringing forth a plan for use of the creational energies that are totally available.

Each of you now has the opportunity to accept or reject these messages and continue to live as a victim of the plans of the enslavers. Or you could change your attitude and accept the possibility that this might be logical truth and something to ponder, consider and then allow the intangible creational life aspect that enlivens each of you to guide you to a decision. The christian bible mentions several times that Mary, mother of Immanuel, pondered things in her heart. In other words, she considered them and "felt" whether those things were true. If something did not fit within the comfort zone of her current understanding, she at least considered it seriously, let the process percolate for a time and then "felt" whether it was true or not. It is suggested that you follow her example and do this in the quiet of prayer time, meditation time or a long quiet walk, then just let things percolate. You will indeed know in your heart if this is an opportunity you want to participate within. Then you must "walk your decision" and take the appropriate steps to change your consciousness, pursue knowledge, live it and acquire wisdom.

Once you each make that decision, there is an entire galactic cheering section that will indeed bring forth-resounding joy and shower you with a loving blessing. You have no idea how much they desire you to know the truth and desire to welcome you back into the evolving focus.

II-16

When the time comes for the beginning of the change over of consciousness through the conversion of the critical number of the necessary percentage, the ripple effect will seem to be unnoticeable. Just as the number of people who now believe that there is interplanetary travel has now reached the critical mass. A remainder still staunchly reject the acceptance of this belief, but that rejection is a shell to protect the rest of their beliefs, for if they are wrong about extraterrestrial visits, then they must entertain the possibility that some or all their beliefs are possibly false. There are compelling reasons that the evidence of these visits has been so vehemently denied by both governmental and religious powers. Yet it provided them with a fear weapon and the temptation to use it as such seduced them into bringing it forth as fanciful entertainment. That earth governments had the abilities to develop the capability was offered in positive possibility within futuristic settings, just as the first attempts to leave the planet itself were idealized. The nonsense of the distortions is indeed ludicrous when viewed in the true picture. However, the truth has escaped their best efforts and it has indeed put a sizable crack in the acceptance of their carefully concocted depiction of who and what mankind is and the cosmology of its existence.

The denial of the existence of anything that has enough people with actual experiences now using the available communications to tell their stories is causing the crumbling of the foundations of the credibility of the whole lie. This was done, not by shocking the population with a big expose, but instead nibbling away at it a little at a time. Now the credibility gap is enough that through this doubt, greater truth is being readily accepted. The truth is that this planned bid for global power was set into motion indeed thousands of years ago. Incredible as it seems when the known "ancient" history is researched and traced back, the plan lays open to discerning minds and is available in print, though the conclusions are not entirely clear. There are no secrets in manifested reality. The further along the evolution of self-aware beings, the more easily situations and other beings are perceived and understood. The temptation to exploit those of lesser evolvement is great indeed in the midst of experience modes between positive and negative experiences. Victim consciousness is the epitome of the negative experience. It draws through the law of attraction like energy, or in other words it draws situations that exploit that consciousness. In acquiring this understanding, it is then obvious that the very first step humanity on this planet must achieve in order to transcend this mode of experience is to shed victim consciousness and regain the self-empowerment mode.

Until the crack in the seemingly "airtight" education of mankind as to his place within the cosmology of the galaxy/universe widens, it is difficult to expect many to accept the truth that the father/god of the past and present is a hoax. This is because first there must be something demonstrable in an experiential fashion that will replace it and it must be the absolute truth! In this process, giving up the victim consciousness through self-empowerment is the beginning step. In order to do this, self-awareness, the ability to consider the individual self over the group loyalty is basic. "Me first" has been exploited through the encouragement of selfish sexual and materialistic practices as a guard to prevent the discovery of this basis of the human expression of who and what manifested life is. When this next fissure in the their foundation becomes a wide enough crack, then the bitter contents of their house of cards will pour forth with repercussions that will lift the human consciousness despite their efforts to enslave it. As the law of attraction works, they draw to themselves like energies/experiences.

The laws of the universe indeed work in mysterious ways to allow for return to balance, while allowing expansiveness through wisdom gained in experience of both the positive and negative expressions. Neither is inactive, both are at play simultaneously thus keeping the balance. During the time spent at the point of balance, all is at rest, just as there is a moment between breaths. During each act of breathing, various functions that are either positive or negative proceed within the body unnoticed because of the governing of the functions of the nerve system in the body. This can be correlated back to the galaxy in comparing the governing system that functions in the fashion of the nervous system.

The human body is a marvelous expression that has the capability of mimicking its source and can function at many levels of holographic and dimensional experience. The gift of an experience within one is to be greatly appreciated and honored. Those beings experiencing in what might be termed older models desire greatly to have the capabilities of your improved one. Thus you have visitors bent on making this happen, but meaning no harm to you. The methodology reflects many of the capabilities theirs lack. For those remembering the experience of interacting with them, this is difficult to accept as reason for these situations. Nonetheless, permission was asked and received at a level of consciousness that is not yet available to their awareness. Those granting this are greatly appreciated for this gift of greater life experience that will be the result. Indeed, there have also been visits from a very much older group that left their unwanted mark long ago and they have been barred from return visits. Any further returns will be with severe repercussions for those individuals for these would be without the approval of their own kind.

This brings forth the previous mention of an extraterrestrial group that are not only assisting the group planning enslavement, but in actuality carry great anger toward this planet. These beings attempted to take over this planet not long after humanity was marooned on it. Not comprehending the warlike genetic alteration, even though they had superior weaponry and control technologies, humanity repulsed them. Retribution has been planned since that long ago time. The control and enslavement plan has been theirs from the beginning. That they come and go and confer with the hierarchy of the planners is kept secret, thus you have secret societies within secret societies. Eternity is a long sequential time, and so they have slowly and carefully laid their plans over many, many years in your counting. The planetary awareness of this presence, which could not be totally hidden, has been translated into "satan or the devil" and thus the tool of fear has been implanted and personified so that you hold it in your consciousness and resist it in a non-reality mode. Those that have been influenced into being the stooges in this long-standing plan reflect the consciousness of those they consider benefactors and they in turn are attracted by the victim stance and consciousness of the rest of humanity. They have not fathomed the plan that is behind the one they are being guided to perpetrate on their fellow humans. If the total plan is allowed by humanity to be completed, the planet may or may not be habitable. Those particular extraterrestrials do not care, so long as they are able to achieve their revenge. Indeed, they are farther out of balance than earth. There is much to be accomplished in the scenario that is playing itself out in these pivotal days that are upon earth and all her inhabitants.

II-17

Through these messages it is hoped that each will strive to verify the inferences made here in brevity. The information is available to verify the historical delineation of the recent (last several thousand) years religious hoax that has been perpetrated. However, this is not to indicate that this was even the beginning. Within this branch of humanity, through the alteration of the DNA/RNA, the inner programmed desire for balance continued to resonate. It was subliminally known that the imbalance was brought about by outside forces, there was then an innate desire that the same outside forces should restore it. There was not conscious memory or records of any kind to indicate who or what had been the source of this imbalance. It was natural for the descendants of this branch of humanity to desire this correction from every outside/extraterrestrial visitor they came into contact with, benevolent or otherwise. This desire was converted over time into deification and worship with ritual religious dogma to support and spread it. The focus of these "religious" formats were both positive and negative, with each attempting to influence the other over time, or worse yet destroy each other. Though the benevolent beings have endeavored to teach the truth and explain each time, their lessons were soon distorted back into the religious dogma of looking for help from outside to rescue mankind from its problem. And so it is at this very moment, accept for those few that have already figured it out are now gleaning the truth from those few who know or from these messages.

Knowing the truth and knowing what to do after the truth is learned is another matter. The universal laws *require* that this branch of mankind must come into understanding and with deliberate focus overcome their victim consciousness through personal responsibility to change their experience. This first step opens the doorway to reentry into the galactic family that they have been separated from for so long. The family is anxious for your return and desires to help in any way that is allowed, but earth's inhabitants must make this first step on its own with only the guidance of its necessity to assist. Then by directly asking for further assistance, more can be given, but even then it cannot be rescued.

It is proper, in light of the above explanation, to address the great as yet unspoken concern about what to do with the over population when this is solved. First of all, there will be a loss of many lives in the chaos that will ensue. Certainly not 5+ billion, but those who refuse to accept the truth will slow down the paradigm project's manifestation. The longer it takes to manifest, the greater the loss of life. Those who refuse to hear and accept after the project completion will be given the opportunity to come into balance in other situations; in other words they will live elsewhere, however this time with full knowledge and accompanied by records. Those who are the new paradigm will then have many choices and opportunities of places to continue their evolution. The members of the ground crew will remember who they really are and are welcome to return to the points of their origin. The balance will be returned, though planet earth will need assistance in returning to health. It will not be as much of a task as might be thought now with the knowledge and techniques available for the asking. The remnant that remains will have interesting times in which to enjoy manifesting the new paradigm into wholeness. No further detail regarding the future will be given until that time arrives. It must be stressed that this is not the phase on which to focus. Until the first step is completed, the last step has no possibility of manifesting. Thus its explanation has been withheld. However, the concern about the overpopulation issue has necessitated this brief explanation. It is important that it be accepted that the future is well encompassed and then set that understanding aside so that the proper emphasis is placed where it belongs. *It belongs on the completion of the first step, individual conscious acceptance of transcending from the victim in need of rescue, into personal responsibility through playing a decisive part in the conception and manifestation of a new paradigm of experience.*

II-18

Through these messages the outline of the status of humanity has been established. Further detail is available to those who desire to investigate beyond what is easily perceived when viewing the media presented information in light of this information. That a hoax of major proportions is being perpetrated is difficult to miss. There is one magic show after another being presented for viewing while the global manipulations continue to restructure national, continental and hemispheric lines of demarcation. The structure of the world as you know it is being dissolved at its very foundations. The plan is at a stage now that it can no longer be prevented. It can yet be sabotaged at specific points to frustrate and slow the process somewhat to give more time in which to reach more people. This material is being distributed at its starting point in the USA, but through the group foci must entail a planetary appeal to be all inclusive of humanity as a whole. The process of the plan is the same and different in every local on the planet. Thus, whether in the vernacular of one country or another, the end result of the plan of planetary slavery is the same. The variety within the human experience must be transcended in order that a true group focus can be attained. The division of ethnicity into race must be dissolved and humanity must consider itself one "race", a word best abandoned for it too reflects emotions that do not serve the birth of the new paradigm. The oneness that is to be sought will transcend the need for identification of diversity. Diversity need not be bred out in order to attain what can only be accomplished within each personal awareness. Appreciation of the opportunity to experience self-awareness manifested into the glory of a human body and evolve through the process of expressing creational energy negates the necessity to delineate personal differences in this way. It is a natural evolution of that awareness.

Appreciation of the gift of self-awareness is understanding that a piece of absolute potentiality that is the sum and substance of the All That Is, is the point of coagulation around which all living things exist. To comprehend it is to honor it and come to understand that it is both fragile and tenaciously committed to evolving through that potentiality that is innate within its very nature. Understanding this simple truth of who and what humanity is has been buried beneath a landslide of superfluous information that has been pushed on mankind to insure distraction and prevent this essential discovery. The distorted need to be fixed, leading to worship of both misunderstood visitors and an imagined outside source for this help, has held the transplanted humans on this planet in a self-created bondage. Many of those who have attained the return to genetic balance remain programmed into the old systems of belief that have failed for thousands of years to achieve the desired goals. It is time for them to awaken and to again experience true human evolvement. It *is the truth* that will set them, *you,* free. When this information is contemplated in the quiet of inner awareness, it will resonate and be known by those who are genetically balanced.

This will raise the question as to whether all those within the same family are automatically genetically balanced. The genes for each are randomly selected at each conception; thus these float within nearly all families at this sequential point. There will be those that are more susceptible to the negative programming that will seem not to carry the gene balance. Again, freewill is freely given. All will be accepted if the realization is sincere even at the last moment. But it is likely that as the initial statement of purpose circulates, the words will resonate and the wakeup call will be answered. The simple few words, translated into all languages, will resound within and in its repetition it will demand an answer within that cannot be denied. The yearning of all the previous generations denied the freedom to evolve is carried at cellular levels and through the genetic release is available when the trigger is activated. It is the response by the first few to this pent up yearning that will bring forth the freedom cry that will begin the wondrous process of the birthing of the new paradigm. It is time now!

The repetitions in the message are meant to offset the continuous barrage of disinformation that has been the foundation of human existence for these thousands of years and now reaches a crescendo as the "second shoe" is nearly ready to be dropped. The emphasis on waking up and accepting the magnitude and duration of the frustrating trip of this branch of humanity down a dead-end path is the essential beginning for changing the conscious perception of this experience. This is then followed by the awareness that this consciousness change is the first layer of the foundation for the new paradigm. Without a firm foundation on the rock of truth, nothing of lasting value can be built.

The next step is either participating in the conception of the beginning statement or the proliferation of it once it is conceived and the further conception of the bare skeleton of what the new paradigm is to become. Not rules and regulations, but what living within it would involve. Dreaming the dream in a sheer playful mode. A rose was created through a play of possibilities. A lily, a monkey, a squirrel, an otter, an elephant were all created in a playful mode of potential possibilities. Man/woman must become child like and consider outlandish and outrageous possibilities until the perfect ideas begin to gel. This is best done within groups with the same intent. Even the most closed will join the *spirit* of the task and often have the most amazing contributions. The host/hostess must set the mood of safety and spontaneity and allow the group to take it from there. Levity opens the door to creativity and the release of true human nature. We are all the children of creation and are set loose to playfully learn who we are and what we are truly capable of doing, governed only by the laws of the universe. It must however, be firmly understood that these do strictly govern, are immutable and every act outside them draws its effects within creation's own, not necessarily sequential, timing. This is known now as divine order.

II-19

The desire to understand the imbalance that followed the original DNA alteration that originated within the natural flow of self contemplation became an abnormal obsession to know for the group of transplanted humans on planet earth. The generations followed one another and their searches within and without failed to give them understanding. The tendency to over respond to all real and misinterpreted threats became the outlet for the desire to understand this imbalance known at the level of intuition. Realizing that this tendency left unbridled would lead to annihilation, religion as an inhibiting factor was introduced. Without the aid of memory or records, it was to provide a historical point of origin as one could best be intuited and to institute some form of control to prevent annihilation. Over sequential time various points of focus were used. The visitation of beings from other planets provided the best possible focus, particularly those who came in attempts to teach and finally to introduce changes in the gene pool as a last resort in their efforts to help this branch of humanity to continue to evolve.

There are two important points of understanding to be made clear. These beings came in benevolence and did not wish to be the object of religious focus. However, the genetic introduction produced offspring that were noticeably more intelligent, but not noticeably less violent if *provoked.* Because of this, these offspring became leaders and usually the focus points or priests of the religious cults. As assisting priests were added, the roles became confused and distorted. Deification of the first of these leaders followed within a few generations of death and various levels of deification of those following happened periodically. Because of their difference, the first-born male of each following generation inherited the leadership role and the task of propagating the perceived change thus creating dynasties of leaders. The remaining progeny intermarried and spread the genetic changes. Because of the focus of male leadership by dominant expression of the aggressive tendency through warfare, females came to be regarded as being of lesser importance accept for the propagation of the male for conquest.

It is important that present day humanity understand its true cosmology. There were what you call indigenous populations already on the planet and evolving through their own natural processes when the transplanted group arrived. The confusion within the efforts of present day scientists trying to create a cosmology from their point of view for the planet is easily understood. They are unable to consider the effects of both types of humans being suddenly present at one point in history and they are unaware of the gene pool additions to the marooned group and the blending of all three ingredients in both the past and the present. This puts them at an extreme disadvantage and their conclusions add only more confusion for an already frustrated branch of humanity. It is necessary to note here that now the indigenous population evolution has been distorted, as few if any remain isolated from proselytizing contacts. Further, the environmental situation includes them within the planetary whole. The aboriginal tribe of Australia no longer propagates and is asking to reincarnate elsewhere in the galaxy. If help is again refused, this will be honored, as they are innocent of any involvement in the chaos forced upon on this planet.

Humanity's roots and how its history has played out, is not important for a delineated timeline, but for an understanding of how the frustration of being marooned was experienced and what far-reaching solutions were tried. Left to deal with their altered genetics humanity has in its confusion refused benevolent help and accepted distorted help. The roots of the refusal and distortion lay within the alteration and its effects that enhanced more than the self-defense aspect. Cooperation became competition, which enhanced greed, lust and the pursuit of power over each other, to name just a few. The knowledge of this history brings forth a fork in the road and with it the decision to continue on the same dead end path or to accept this offer of help that is again being made. For those willing to comprehend the plans for the present path, it would seem the choice would be easy.

However, the ingrained programming of looking for rescue rather than accepting the responsibility of making the necessary changes requires leaving behind a long established comfort zone.

To literally climb out of the morass of confusion to a point of overview, observe the struggling masses expending their energy swimming upstream against the flow of creative energy because of a false perception of who and what they are through misconceptions and misinformation, takes courage. It is not an easy opportunity to accept and requires a commitment to this very personal process. It involves separating from the mass conscious belief systems in order to contemplate what is true and then adopting a new concept of personal truth.

Fortunately, this has already been accomplished by a surprising number of individuals. These, not knowing the history, through an instinctual awareness that there was a hidden story, relentlessly pursued their need to know. What came to be known was perceived despite the fact that what long-standing truth was known, was withheld except to the few planners. The current *magical/technological* cover-up continues with regard to these truths as well as the planned enslavement of all but the elite planners. Difficult as it will be for those of the Judaic/Christian heritage to accept, their cosmological story was deliberately written in a distorted form utilizing written records later conveniently hidden or destroyed and utilizing what was believed to be myths. (Little known published scientific research reveals through translations of written records these myths were actual oral history passed from one generation to the next for hundreds of years.) This deliberately distorted cosmology was compiled at the beginning of the planned scenario as it plays out today.

When a genetically altered teacher was born within this religious focus and instructed with truth, he suffered a planned near death and escaped to another part of the planet. Believing him dead, deification soon followed. The distortion of those teachings was almost immediate, in order that the plan being laid and yet to manifest in wholeness, might not be derailed. This genetically enhanced human's personal choice for this mission was to teach personal responsibility.

This has brought forth the imposing question of what to do about changing the outcome at this late stage in the sequence of happenings leading to the planned future that is nearly incomprehensible to humanity. Thus a second layer of entreaties for help was begun by a small unorganized group of conscious awareness on this planet, one that was/is answerable. We have now returned to the present moment in our consideration of an encapsulated history of earth's human population.

II-20

The avenue of entry into the minds and most important of all, the hearts of humanity lies not so much through logic as through the emotions. The great playing card of the deceptive plan has been the emotion of fear. Subliminal guidance is the first layer of control, then more layers are added to achieve control of whatever focus is desired. The last and most effective leverage of all is fear. Fear is the most creative of thought forms in the negative aspect. Love is the most creative in the positive expression. The reason these are at the top of the scale in the human focus is the rate of the vibration of emotion that accompanies each. The degree in which the human can experience these depends upon the range in which each has experienced them. Thus you can understand the reason for the deliberate proliferation of horror, war and gangster type movies. These have been deliberately promoted for the express purpose of increasing the experiencing range of fear. Those films that pass for "love" experiences usually contain great feelings of remorse and sadness as well as more subtle experiences of fear. The technological societies of the planet have little experience with what true love really is. Fed a diet of sexual based unfulfilling relationships as love, it is no surprise that family life has reached a disastrous level for so many. Every negative aspect is paraded as the norm. Just as each individual is a human becoming, so also each relationship and family is a entity becoming, formed by the combination focus of the 2 or more included within it. With no agreed upon ideal purpose and few of the character traits necessary to carry each through the experience, the only answer seems to be the experience of a stream of beginnings and endings.

In contrast, those who have had what is called near death experiences return to their conscious realities with regret for having to return and an overwhelming experience of what they term love. These were experiences of the energies that emanate through the creative focus that maintains and expands this galaxy. It is, when analyzed, if that is even possible, the action of the universal laws to their full extent: attraction, intention and allowance resulting in the harmony of balance. This focus is supported by an even greater focus of these laws in action. It is the added presence of harmony that seems so intensely pleasant in those brief experiences.

It is not difficult for each to be in the experience of the negative situations that are there at every turn in the search for respite from stressful living. One needs only to close the eyes and check the true feelings in the midst of an adventure movie to know these inner feelings are not harmonious. It is the balancing experience of the opposite, the harmonious vibration of creation that brought forth each self-aware conscious entity and maintains each and all through a continuing focus of that same energy, that is overwhelmed by deliberate diversion from it. This is not because this marvelous energy isn't available; it is that the conscious awareness is too cluttered to find the quiet space within to experience it. If it cannot be even slightly experienced, how indeed can it be drawn in, (attracted), and focused into expression and a greater experience of it. In order to truly experience it, it must flow through the conscious awareness and be refocused into the rebirth of greater expression. In other words, to know love it must be attracted, encompassed and expressed outwardly through both acknowledgement and outward transference of it. In this process it is magnified and flows with the creative expression. That is how each comes into being and creates the opportunity to become.

The sexual romantic hugging and kissing "love" that has been programmed as love is not the love that creates and maintains physical galaxies and uncountable beings becoming. Just as the word god conjures up all kinds of negative reactions because of its false and confusing uses and is best avoided thus the word love has been avoided within these messages. Instead "flow of creative energies, etc.," has been substituted. The people who have had near death experiences return to conscious awareness with a true understanding of the feeling experience that the word love was intended to convey. Brief glimpses of it are experienced. Sometimes, but not always, a mother's first experiences with a new baby; couples who have shared long lives together reach that level of regard for each other; there are rare appreciative times of nature to name a few. These are intense moments of an emotional/vibratory level that is called enlightenment or ecstasy. These are so strange and unfamiliar to most of the humans on this planet that the few able to attain and maintain it become "saints" if this state of empowerment becomes known. It is the level at which manifestation of thought is so natural that seemingly impossible feats are accomplished. It is, compared to the norm on this planet, "super-consciousness." However, in other human experiences on other planets, it is normal life expression.

The point of this discussion is an attempt to explain to a small degree what mankind on this planet is missing out on. What you are experiencing as manifested life, is a poor substitute for what it was intended to be. What is being offered is an opportunity to take advantage of a doorway of "grace", an offer of a favor, a special dispensation. Accepting this will allow the opportunity to bridge the gap of lost normal evolvement that should have been accomplished in the time spent in this dead end experience. This is available to all mankind on this planet, not just those transplanted humans. The effects of intervention and denial of freewill choice ripple outward and the sequential results are not known. Even this special privilege may bring effects that are not anticipated though careful consideration has been given before making this privilege available. If the inhabitants of earth choose not to accept the opportunity, then it is a moot point.

Those that have sat through hours and hours of teaching/preaching within religious institutions may find some of these messages reminiscent of those experiences. These are not meant to be so. These are meant to bring as many considerations as possible before the conscious awareness in order that the focus of thought may be guided through a decision process that will allow for logical conclusions and commitment that will not be regretted. The commitment to the birthing of a new paradigm requires courage and tenacity, for the time of chaos is necessary. As long as that which does not serve this branch of humanity's evolvement remains in tact, it is impossible to birth something of total newness. Chaos, order, chaos followed by a new form of order is the flow of creation. It is creation living itself, for creation is aware and is life.

II-21

There is a point of personal decision that must be reached by each individual that chooses to become involved in this project. It must be understood that once the commitment is made, it will change the perspective, the way in which the experience of situations and relationships are comprehended. If the commitment is real, it will be as if you are observing from a greater perspective. It will be as if there is a split reality. The daily experience will be the same, yet an observational dimension will seem to be added. The observation mode will be experienced as an ability to understand how various past and present knowledge and experience fit into a fluid puzzle picture. There will be a realization that reality as known has changed. It will be observed that the pieces of the puzzle are not firm and do not come together into a recognizable static picture. Instead the pieces are of a gelatinous nature and are moving and flowing in constantly changing patterns. In the perception of this process, it is then possible to conceive that certain rigid insertions cause the ebb and flow to be influenced to form rigid dam like structures restricting the freedom of the natural flow. If maintained within the human individual flow of changing patterns, this brings on the end of the experience, as the life force must continue to express in a free flowing fashion, or it is withdrawn. This is also true within a larger group concept.

When it is possible to encompass this concept of the elementary need to express that is at the very essence if creation, then it can be understood that the halting of this flow of progress and any plan to reverse it causes chaos. Within the mind's eye it is like a flow of multiple artists' colors flowing together and yet staying separate and spreading out. At one place, the colors are moving in a slow swirl and beginning to coagulate and intermingle in a darkening manner that is not consistent. As the watcher observes from the over-view position, it is apparent that this coagulated point cannot stop the flow that is moving all around it. The flow will continue to move around it and leave it behind. If the consistency of this coagulated energy can be softened, it can again rejoin the flow.

The job of softening and dissolving this dark and coagulated energy is the object and purpose of these messages. If the beliefs of the mass consciousness of this planet can be changed and a new paradigm of experience conceived and accepted the dark and coagulated energies will dissolve and the expansive flow of creation will be restored.

Within the flow of creation, the knowledge that is lived into wisdom moves through stages of what is truth within the vibrational/dimensional realms of experience. As knowledge becomes wisdom, then these conceptual lines of delineation are surpassed and the old concepts are outdated and no longer applicable. As transplanted humanity became aware that something must curb their over stimulated aggressive tendencies, religion was conceptualized. With the genetic balance returned, now it is time for those humans to leave this concept behind and begin to conceptualize the causative factors that brought them into manifested experience. They must conceive on the larger scale what it is that maintains not only their individual focus but also the larger focus of the galactic environment of their life. It is time to return to citizenship on a grander scale. All of this must be bitten off, chewed and digested in a very large bite. Why so quickly? Two reasons: first, all previous opportunities to do this were refused. Secondly, sometimes the medicine in one large bitter pill is more effective than all the small ones.

II-22

When the transition begins to take place within each individual consciousness there will be a literal rebirth as the awareness is released into a new sphere. The acceptance of the reality of multiple layers of endeavor that are operating simultaneously with multiple agendas is the first step of entering greater dimensional living. The personal reality is enveloped within local, regional, state, national and global realities that are each focused on greater agendas and are each a more encompassing reality. It is the purpose of the purposeful negative planners to encompass and blend these multiple realities into one blended focus with one agenda, theirs. Mankind can avoid participation in an experience of a collapsing dimensional reality by creating its own new experience within the negative plan. It is possible to do this through participation of the creation of the new paradigm. Each may participate in bringing forth its unknown and yet to be created layers of encompassing new realities. Without the knowledge of the magnitude and power of this project the negative planners cannot prevent it, if the desire, commitment and resolve to bring it forth is present and active in the necessary number of humans. There is no way they can control a human's ability to focus on the creation of a new reality, unless that human allows their thought process to be overwhelmed. Granted it will take commitment and resolve, but the potentiality to do this is present in all, accept those with advanced brain deterioration.

Those beings would include those with advanced Alzheimer's (It is interesting to note the honoring of a dis-ease by capitalization.), those that have "fried" their brain cells with excessive drug abuse and those with particular birth defects. Again, it is noted that the freewill choices of life style will have end results that must be accepted. How these choices play out remain unknown to others. Each must answer to or be rewarded for these within their own lifetime review. The choice to transcend experience into wisdom is always available, but it must be a true realization accompanied by a shift in attitude and deed. It must be remembered that the universal law of attraction works. The clarification and understanding of the nuances these laws encompass much understanding. The opportunity to know of and understand the application of these could be greatly enhanced by the teaching of enlightened beings who would walk among you, if invited and when it is safe for them to do so. There is a spiritual law book available, but the study of it must not interfere with the focus on the manifestation of the new paradigm. Without the framework of a new paradigm within which to experience the understanding and use of these laws in practical reality, it would be difficult for earth's humanity as a whole to experience these truths. It is necessary to begin at a practical beginning point.

It is within possibility for those who are reading these messages to begin to contemplate the action of the first two laws of the universe within their life experience to this time. The law of like drawing likes sometimes looks like opposites attracting as in the case of relationships. However on deeper understanding when reviewed in wisdom further along in the duration of the experience, more similarity than difference is usually discovered. The ability to deliberately attract the experience or lack of the experience of material manifestation into being through purposeful thought and endeavor supports the awareness of the second law. The law of allowance is more difficult to perceive because of the degree of control exercised individually and by outside psychological (including religious) and technological mind manipulations. It is indeed, difficult for most of mankind to actually have and/or maintain a sovereign attitude. The opportunity to live life with freedom of choice and be *allowed* to observe and learn from the results of those choices is rare. To declare the desire to do so is incorporated within the desire for a new paradigm of experience.

The choice to participate in the creation of the new paradigm must not involve commitment to enslavement by another set of rules and regulations that simply control in a different way. That would not be a new paradigm. Herein lies the difficulty of transcending what exists and conceptualizing an entirely different framework of experience. It is only the statement of purpose that is necessary. It must then be followed by a slim, concise outline. Fleshing it out will be the adventure of the new future. A very *basic* outline will not seem to be enough but if more is attempted it will be contaminated with the concepts of the present. Surely mankind has had enough of the same old, same old simply repackaged and that always has produced physical and spiritual indigestion.

Repetitions again! These are to keep the focus where it is intended. First focus on the individual consciousness transition from victim to victor. It is the victor that writes the history. This time, do not bother to write the history of the past, for it is what it is, and there will be no time to care. It is time to move on. This time it is the victor that will write the history of the future. These messages and this project are gifts to earth's humankind, from their galactic brothers and sisters, to help ensure it is they that write their own future and not the enslavers. The question is, will the gifts be accepted and acted on by enough of humanity to change the unpleasant future planned to manifest in the very near future? Your decision is awaited with great love and caring. All the help possible is given at all times for the asking. Only when you are able to ask from the greater perspective of the victory of control of your own consciousness can physical help be given, not on an individual basis, but to the planet and its inhabitants as a whole.

II-23

With each sequential chapter of the experience of the transplanted humans on this planet the results of every effort to counteract the genetic variation has seemed to end in futility. However, that is the perception from "inside the forest" so to speak. The introduction of a normal human DNA/RNA structure to earth's human gene pool allowed a correction to spread by random selection through the subsequent generations. Hundreds of years have gone by as this effective genetic process has gone through its natural sequence. What appears to be a long time in your counting within creations orderly process is merely the blinking of an eye in the larger picture. Those indigenous groups that have been included in the intermixing process by choice or otherwise have received both genetic alterations, causing uninvited changes in their archetypal evolutionary pattern. This points out the consequences that ripple outward when the will of one group is forced upon another. Even though an individual may make a freewill choice, the effects for the generations that follow are influenced in ways that are not perceived at the time of the initial decision. The intentional changing of the genetic structure of a large group is a slow process, but as the change begins to manifest, it then spreads at an exponential rate.

It must be acknowledged that the return to the genetic norm has not manifested in an even pattern through out the planet. Not all groups with the altered genetic pattern have accepted the introduced gene resource at the same rate. Social and religious bias has influenced this because of the prevention of intermarriage with other groups, thereby locking out the introduced positive genetic change. This has allowed a considerable number of beings to remain locked in the more aggressive pattern. Many of these are deeply involved in the negative enslavement focus. It must be pointed out here very strongly, that this does *not* indicate that there are superior and inferior groups. Within creation, many diverse experiences of evolvement are allowed. If that type of "judgement" existed, then where indeed would earth's population be within the total scale of evolvement? Certainly not in an enviable place! Any feelings of superiority can be put in their place by raising the question for the necessity of the whole of the galaxy to be concerned with the plight of this planet because of the consciousness of its inhabitants! Be very, very careful in understanding these particular explanations. No judgment is intended, only brief overview lessons in understanding the situation of all the people of the planet.

Certainly among all the groups there are what can be termed progressive and regressive genes. Through the random process of available gene combinations at conception it is possible for the most aggressive being, with the appropriate partner, to procreate a genetic opposite in the next generation. It has been happening since the project was started. It is how the situation has changed and has reached the present point with a now possible influence of the planetary future. Had the genetic selection process been apparent at the conscious level, then the introduced genes to modify the aggressive tendencies would have been promptly bred out for the purposes of warfare and continuation in the confines of aggression for the transplanted human group would have been assured.

The complexity of the universal laws increase, as they are understood. Moving through the understanding of the laws of attraction and focused intentional manifestation to the law of allowance adds complexity at each level for all are interactive. Application of the law of allowance opens the door to experience the flow of creative energy. It might be said that it is "love in action." What is called patience is allowance. Here a nuance must be understood. There is a difference between tolerance and patience. The difference can best be described by the emotion that is felt. This is an especially fruitful opportunity for self-contemplation. Tolerance carries an emotional charge of resentment while patience is usually accompanied by heartfelt anticipation, even amusement, by the observer. There is a very profoundly observable difference between tolerance and patience. This is a difference that can be observed and intentionally changed in mid-stream, so to speak. It is this type of conscious decision that promotes the transcendence of knowledge into wisdom through the conscious choice to rise above one emotion into the other by giving up an attitude and an opinion. With out releasing what is causing the resentment, no transition of attitude can be made. In the human experience, it is noted that release of tolerance into patience is often accompanied by physical smiling. An indication of just how good it feels to allow the creational flow to express through human experience.

It is hoped those who spread these messages remember to be patient with their fellow humans, for there will be much rejection in the beginning. The comfort zone of deeply ingrained programming is difficult to soften. A great deal of seeding must be done. Even though rejected, the seed ideas will remain and await the triggering that will cause them to root and grow. What the triggers are will be unknown, for all are unique to each conscious awareness. The seeds need not be full explanations, but for many only what appear to be chance remarks can be accepted in the moment. Just that much is doing your job well, for it is critical to sense what is and is not appropriate. Too much locks the door before it opens even a crack.

The christian religion has employed the most aggressive proselytizing program in the history of the planet. If the founding teacher of the distorted christian faith had been allowed to complete his teaching to its potential, and had it been spread with the zeal of the christian focus, then marvelous progress would have been made. Nonetheless, the members have applied the first two universal laws relentlessly without understanding them. Through contemplation of this point, much about the use and misuse of these two laws can be learned. With *discernment,* "a few" of these applications could be applied to the advancement of the new paradigm; certainly the "never give up" aspect of their approach.

II-24

It is appropriate to mention again the fact that there is among earth's population those who have volunteered to pause in their personal evolvement process and place their progress in jeopardy. This has been purposefully done to assist earth's inhabitants to make the long overdue transition out of isolation and back into greater evolvement and involvement with their galactic brothers, sisters and cousins. These have assumed the same bodies with the same random genetic physical expressions that each conscious awareness on earth assumes at birth. Their motivations for doing this are as varied as the experiences that allowed them their personal evolvement. In general it may be assumed that the benefits to earth and her inhabitants was considered worth the risk of the loss of their progress should the opportunity again be rejected. If earth's inhabitants choose to remain stuck in their current pattern of experience, these beings will remain within that destiny. The risk is also a great motivator.

There are two reasons for these messages. The first is to awaken the volunteers and answer invocations for help. The second is to provide the focus for the birth of this new paradigm of human experience for which these evolved beings were willing to take such great risk. It is for you to know that successful deeds of valor do not go without reward. It is not at all "egotistical" for each one that reads this material to give careful consideration as to whether or not they are one of the "visiting" volunteers. To ponder this possibility is wise indeed. Knowingness within will govern awareness of the truth of this possibility and allow consideration of the risk of ignoring it insofar as what that could mean in the larger picture. Whether or not this is a person's truth, to aid in offering the opportunity for humanity to change its future and return to its rightful place within the creative flow of evolvement, is reason enough to <u>volunteer now</u> as a member of the ground crew. Creative thought is not limited to any one group, but is inherent within *all* self-aware consciousness. It is called becoming!

Certainly the volunteers do not place their earned progress in jeopardy to simply acknowledge it. They volunteer to assist their fellow humans to move beyond this present mode of experience. Each brings their special successful experiencing techniques as a contribution to the birth and launching of the new paradigm of experience. The logical way to help humanity to conceive of this new mode of experience is to participate within the present one so that it can be understood. In the midst of the chaos of imbalance, all volunteers have the ability to purposefully remember aspects of recent balanced experience and give guidance with regard to these aspects in the conception of the purpose and outline for the new experience desired by earth's inhabitants. These first volunteers are one part of the answer to the prayers and supplications for help that have been focused to "god". The new volunteers attracted to this process and joining with equal commitment are the return flow of invested energy, reflecting the exchange that is the dynamic operative quality of creation. It is the law of attraction in action. As the law of intentional creation, through the two steps of birthing the new paradigm, is added to the attraction process, vibratory intensity increases and transformation toward manifestation into perceivable reality begins.

It is necessary for all volunteers to consider, contemplate and decide to accept the truth of who and what each one is and then move on into the fuller completion of each assigned segment. The first step is to spread the knowledge of the opportunity to create a new paradigm of experience, keeping the concept simple, simple, simple!!! Gently inform and encourage many to change their consciousness from victim to victor through the knowledge that thought has the power to change manifested creation. Creation expresses in all experience, situations and circumstances as well as "things". Each thought, word and deed through attitudes and beliefs structures everyone's experience.

Each person every day is surrounded with many opportunities to offer a different perspective or a word of encouragement that assists the knowledge and understanding of this basic concept. This is planting the seeds for changes in the mass consciousness. This may seem a small way to begin this extraordinary change, but once begun in this people to people manner it will build at an exponential rate. Many are ready and waiting to respond positively now to carry and spread the change. These will be receptive because the present mode of life expression just doesn't seem right, but no ideas resonate within them for what to do about this knowingness. There is only a sense of being overwhelmed by the immensity of their situation and the presence of these discordant inner feelings. These moments are the opportunities to begin to walk the path of your impending new future. Plant seeds at every opportunity. As you do, you will attract more opportunities to do so. Now is the sequential moment to stand in the reality of who and what you are and begin to experience the reason for being in this body on this planet at this moment. The alarm clock is ringing. It is time to wake up and begin living in the joy of creating the new future.

II-25

It is well known among the people on the planet that the time of chaos that has long been predicted appears to be manifesting into reality. These predictions were purposefully implanted in some of the religious teachings. However, the indigenous tribes long ago taught similar predictions clearly defining this time frame. That appears to make both coincide. The difference is that some of these predictions were promulgated for a purpose and those of the indigenous people are genuine prophecies. Their prophecies contain identifiable time frame predictions (The Mayan calendar for example, calculates/prophesying the end of the current 26,000 year cycle as ending on December 12, 2012.) while those of deliberate intent to induce fear assured those that hear them the exact time cannot be known. This enables them to use various sets of conditions as indications of their possible manifestation and through the years to manipulate the believers over and over again. American Indian prophecies tell of a time of chaos to be followed by the time of the "rainbow man". Zuni Indian art contains depictions of a rainbow man in anticipation of that future event. It is the purpose of these messages to bring that prophecy to fruition.

That which has been and is judged as "pagan" often contains portions of truth when the analogies are understood through wisdom. There is no one perfect way to truth for all of mankind, for each must create his or her own path. This does not indicate that wisdom through knowledge applied is not available within a group approach, as long as the focus is open and searching. When a group focus becomes locked in rigid dogma it becomes a whirlpool and not a flow within the expansive creative focus. It is to be remembered that other than the universal laws, what appears to be absolutely true often must be transcended as the knowledge experienced becomes wisdom. At that point, new applicable knowledge becomes available to experience into wisdom, and the old concepts no longer apply. The first time this is experienced in a lifetime, it can be traumatic. The individual is faced with the decision of whether to stay with what has brought him/her to the familiar point of understanding and remain in the whirlpool or let go and move on in the process of evolvement. Many of those who have sincerely searched in this lifetime have often experienced wisdom gained, followed by boredom and soon begin new quests for knowledge. Those who have grown from early childhood into maturity within the indoctrination of a single religious focus may find opening to a wider perspective through these messages as emancipation or find themselves in shocked dismay. Each who allow time to ponder both points of view in their hearts will come to a knowing of what is true for them and act accordingly. It is hoped that those of both points of view will practice allowance. It is certainly to be practiced by the volunteers. All are humans becoming. "Help us to become!"

The vision of the "Rainbow Man" and the anticipation of his

coming can be interpreted two ways. Those of the christian viewpoint could assume it means the return of Jmmanuel (Jesus) or it could indicate the advent of a wiser and emancipated human population on earth. Certainly it will require a wiser group to bring forth the new paradigm of human experience, thus the prophecy would seem quite clear. However, it could also indicate both as true. It would require an open minded and far less aggressive human focus for Jmmanuel to walk again among his human brothers and sisters in safety. The distortions of his teachings would make it impossible for those indoctrinated in the current beliefs to recognize and accept him for who and what he is because of their current understandings and expectations.

The picture of the rainbow man/woman is an easy visualization to hold in mind for a depiction of the anticipated personal experience within the new paradigm. It is important that meaningful symbology be adopted in order that the new paradigm become real in the minds of the those who desire this transcendence process to become a reality. It could represent the consciousness change from victim to victor through attitude and thought adjustment and a resting point in the midst of the confusion of change. This transition in how life is experienced will not come about without bringing about some internal chaos within personal experience. This will be preparation for that which will manifest on a larger scale as this concept takes root and grows within the mass consciousness for it is a reversal in the direction of the journey of mankind. It might be compared to walking down a long flight of stairs with a large group of people, changing your mind half way down, turning around and going back up through them. When enough people also change their minds and start going back up, it won't be as difficult. However, for the ground crew, who are the first to begin this process, it will take purposeful intent with resolve to accomplish this feat. Picturing this process in the mind's eye allows for the understanding that volunteering for this mission requires much dedicated involvement to plan, organize and arrive at the picnic for rainbow people.

As you listen to the media presentations, the theme of resistance to perceived wrong doers and evil manifestations of disease, etc., for example, is spelled out as the "war on poverty, the war on drugs or the war on "?" It is amazing to observers that citizens have not realized that there is yet to be one stance *against* that has produced effective results. It does however provide a way to extort *your* money out of your pockets directly and from your national treasury. Among your common sayings are many truisms. "What you resist persists." It is encouraged that the volunteers observe this truism at work within their personal and the national experience. It is preparation for a basic consciousness transition.

II-26

The law of allowance is the most difficult of the three active or dynamic universal laws to accept as necessary and to practice. It is essential to understand the law of attraction in order to apply the law of allowance. The composite of thoughts, opinions and attitudes of each individual generate the experience patterns of living. Through the flow of daily experiences these are filtered through this composite of each one's total collective experience. In this way the pattern or matrix is in a dynamic and fluid process. When attitudes and opinions are deliberately programmed within a limited set of rigid guidelines, the activity level of the total pattern of experience begins to slow. The key is the word deliberately. This means that the guidelines are imposed, not by the individual through knowledge experienced into wisdom but by the beliefs imposed on the individual by those he/she considers outside authorities. The pattern of each individual as a whole *attracts* to itself life experiences that resonate in harmony with that pattern. If a person desires some thing or some experience that does not resonate with that pattern, it is difficult, if not impossible to attract it. Two divergent patterns cannot blend cohesively.

For example, there are few within the "modern societal norm" that do not know at least one man or woman that in the scenario of several marriages repeats the same pattern of abused/abuser relationships. The pattern of the victim draws the abuser, whether physical or verbal, no matter how many times a new partner enters the picture. This is especially true if the relationships quickly follow each other. The pattern of experience is held in place by the thoughts, attitudes and opinions that are at the basis of self-awareness. The victim desires to be rescued. Someone or some event must come and change their life. If however, there is time taken to consider and contemplate the elements of the situation resulting in changes of attitude and opinion (knowledge to wisdom) the pattern of experience can change.

The tragedy of religious teachings of an outside primal source as a personified rescuer is that it not only instills a victim consciousness, but also feeds it. A victimized personified deity hanging on a cross as a status of veneration draws to those believers what they venerate, the victim experience. If poverty is venerated, poverty is attracted. If hard work is venerated, then life will be filled with hard work. If killing is venerated, then death is attracted. What ever the dominant focus of thought, attitude, and opinion, is will influence the overall matrix and dominate the attraction of experience.

A child is born into its family situation, or lack of one, in innocence, except for inherited genetic coding. It is totally influenced in its experience by the same thoughts, attitudes and opinions of its parents until it is old enough to begin to attract some of its own experiences. Eventually it graduates to its own field of attraction, but the pattern of its matrix is already present. The direct influence of the family is present to the degree of acceptance of those thoughts, attitudes and opinions by the maturing individual. The physical attributes present also contribute to the attitudes that develop during the maturation process. Parental, teacher and peer influences all play their part. More layers of influence are present. The thoughts, attitudes and opinions of groups input to the individual matrix. Identities within ethnic, neighborhood, city, region, state, nation, etc, add their influence. Next add the conscious and subconscious programming by radio, TV, movies, newspapers, magazines, and on-line information. Each of these composite patterns is received and filtered through thought, opinion and attitude to create the individual resonating matrix.

As the overall life experience for a major portion of the inhabitants of the planet becomes measurably more complex, the matrix designs have become less defined. The resulting confusion and overwhelm being experienced has become more intense reflecting this lack of matrix definition. This appears as self-absorption as each attempts to stay focused within the vagueness of their indefinite pattern. The resulting feelings of overwhelm and lack of definition allows for the planners of dark deeds to tighten the noose of creeping enslavement literally before the eyes of the victims without their notice. Those awake and awakening are incredulous that the situation has reached this ludicrous degree.

Through understanding this overview of the combined and individual experience of mankind on planet earth, it would appear that the solution of this deteriorating human experience would logically be to give it up in its present form and replace the complexity with simplicity. How can this be accomplished? Refer to the "Handbook for The New Paradigm" for directions. "When all else fails, read the directions." An apropos truism!

II-27

The universal laws, though appearing simple in concept, contain many nuances that appear as paradoxes. A paradox is "a statement that seems contradictory, etc. but may be true in fact; a statement that is self-contradictory, and, hence, false" as quoted from Webster's New World dictionary. For example, the law of allowance is not a law unless upheld by the laws of attraction and intentional creation. In this case then, the law of allowance is a paradox. It is and is not a law. Inasmuch as the underlying basis of creation is conceptional thought, the laws are concepts to be interpreted or applied within the parameters of each and the combination of all. In the simplest terms possible, this means that as each is understood, it must also be understood that all act in cooperation bringing forth the result of harmony and balance. The 4th law depends on the interaction of the previous three as a prerequisite. Personal and group awareness acts as a form of clearinghouse for these fundamental components of creation. Without firm guidelines for expression, creation would express only as incomprehensible chaos. Attempting to comprehend the underlying laws of creation within their continuous interacting flow as they delineate creation is something like wondering which came first, the chicken or the egg. THE CREATION SIMPLY IS! It is to be comprehended and joined cooperatively at the point of realization to the best of each one's ability to do so. What ever that is, is "good enough!"

It is logical then to come to the understanding that evolvement within creation is a constantly exchanging cooperative process of knowledge and experience toward wisdom. Those three words can be exchanged for attraction, intention and allowance. The inclusion of new information within the belief system allows for changes in thoughts, opinions and attitudes. This then begins the process of becoming knowledge applied because the matrix or pattern of the individual or group changes and attracts different experiences. Through the trial and error process experience sooner or later becomes understanding and the cycle repeats. Creation and its processes are all logical. Thought thinking could function in no other mode that would manifest and maintain form. Emotion is an important ingredient within the process. However, when, in the individual or group experience, it runs the show, emotion then becomes a trap and indicates a correctable imbalance. It indicates the necessity of setting aside time for self-contemplation and "pondering in the heart" to determine the truth of the information, situation or circumstance that triggers the emotional reaction. It is important to determine what indeed is the reason for the emotion. When the comfort zone must be defended, it may be too rigidly maintained. Perhaps it is the time to consider letting go and getting back into the flow. That which assaults the comfort zone of the belief system can often times contain the elements for moving to the next level of evolvement and deserves consideration. Considering and looking for the logic within the whole of the issue or situation is participating within the 3 steps of basic creation, leading to the 4th.

Inertia is not an energetic element; therefore it results in either termination of the focus or causes a void that will be filled with something. It is best if it is filled intentionally. The object is to be charismatic within the process of participating in creation. Each is a focused point of self-awareness within the entirety of creation. This is not an insignificant status. There is no such thing as being "just a human being"! Underlying all of creation, including the universal laws, is pure potentiality. As a focused self-aware component of the whole, the potentiality of that whole belongs to each and every component. Each is "entitled" to equal access to that potentiality by simply applying it, indeed by becoming it. What that potentiality is for each individual or group, is a matter of choice governed only by current genetic limitations and thoughts, opinions and attitudes. Therefore, thoughts, attitudes and opinions govern how much advantage is taken of the absolute potentiality that is yours by right of who and what you are. Those that have progressed beyond the earth experience by availing themselves of this opportunity to become have been called "gods". That which they "have done, you can do also and more." It is your already owned entitlement. It is time to stop listening to the falsehoods of the need to wait until after-death to claim your heritage. Is yours now, and always has been. The knowledge of who and what you are allows you to apply the laws by which you were birthed into the creational flow, and to become your dreams. It is your right to live life abundantly.

Among the nuances of the application of the laws is the necessity to understand that it is necessary to live *"within"* the laws. It is within the law of allowance that it is appropriate to discuss abundance and luxury. A dictionary often contains much wisdom and is most helpful in reaching greater understanding. According to Webster's New World Dictionary, abundance is "great plenty, more than enough." Luxury is "the enjoyment of the best and most costly things, anything contributing to such enjoyment, usually something not necessary." Therefore abundance is living within the law of allowance for it allows all to also live in abundance. Luxury encompasses living in extraordinary abundance. It is also *very important* to emphasize that abundance is not necessarily the same thing to each becoming focus of awareness! It is the responsibility of each one in the process of becoming to manifest their life experience within their own ability to function within the laws. However, it is not within the laws to take another's abundance to add to your own. Cooperation is the keynote and competition is the death knell of progress. Does that mean its unfitting to win a race or participate in athletic events or to be better at something than others? Of course not, it is just that the perspective is required to fit *"within"* the application of the universal laws. This is an example of the paradox principle that can easily become a trap.

The path of becoming is like your game of golf, not at all predictable in every aspect or the ability to always repeat success. There in lies the challenge and the fascination of the game. In the game of life, there is no dropping out. Once focused into awareness, the game is on going. It may change playing fields, but it keeps on keeping on. It is much easier to play if that concept is firmly held in mind. The more playful the attitude and the greater the sense of humor that is brought into the process, the easier the passage through becomes. Indeed, those who have trod the path before you laugh well and frequently. Try it, you will like it.

II-28

It is through the probabilities of acceptance of the material contained in these messages that the focus point of the change in mass consciousness is focused. The new paradigm of human experience is based upon a multi-faceted campaign to assist mankind to bring about the much-needed completion of this phase of experience. If indeed what is called reincarnation is true and if the aboriginal tribe in Australia can request to be reincarnated on another planet, why isn't it possible for the genetically corrected portion of the transplanted segment of humanity to do this? The answer lies in the degree of knowledge lived into wisdom. Those particular people are well aware of their connection to creation and have learned to live in harmony with nature. They are watching their young people being seduced by modern technology, what they consider beliefs not lived into wisdom and see their progress earned slipping away. Their beliefs and what is judged as a meager existence in the judgment of modern societies is to them wholeness and abundance lived in peace and harmony. It is a matter of perspective.

The point is, where within "religion driven societies" is progress in applying the basic universal laws? Where is harmony with nature and living in peace with one another in the modern technological society? Is it possible to ever learn those lessons within the focus of the centuries upon centuries of on going genetic and learned behavior? It does not appear so to those charged with the task of observing the process. So again your brothers/sisters offer helping hands for they truly care about you and desire to see you return to the family of evolving humanity. It is truly said of mankind on earth, if something doesn't work, they just seem to do more of it.

Indeed, it is true that there are some of what you call aliens that are instigating your situation and fully cooperating with the dark planners on your planet. But they are closely related to the basic group of planners also through genetic addition. Is earth the only planet out of balance? No, as it has been mentioned before, this segment of creation, this galaxy, that is the realm of focus included in these messages, experiences the expansiveness of the creative flow through the energetics of positive and negative experiences. Like disease in your bodies, a level of great imbalance can spread and thus a cure is sought. In the case of earth, surgery is not the recommended cure. It is preferred that the holistic method of changing thoughts, attitudes and opinions create a renewal and a new paradigm of experience. This would allow mankind to rejoin the creative flow through transcending this experience rather than stubbornly continuing on the wheel of repetition until they do complete the transition individually and collectively farther down the sequential time frame.

The situation on this planet, as confusing as it is to comprehend, is as it is. It is important to grasp the reality and the seriousness of the consequences of it continuation, but the focus of importance is on creating the change. It will not be found through continued observation of the imbalance, but in placing the focus on what is desired to replace it. There is no other way to move through it and into what is desired. Again it is important to stress the need to accept that the belief systems now present within the mass awareness of the planet have *not* lead humanity out of it dilemma. These have mired it more deeply than ever in the situation now leading it to the lowest ebb yet of this human experience. If it hasn't worked in the past, and it doesn't work now, then it is time to accept that, open the belief system to different ideas and ponder their truth rather than reject them without consideration.

When enough are reached and the truth of the above analysis is accepted, then the spread of the change out of victim consciousness will begin in earnest. At a particular exponential rate, the mass consciousness will accept this understanding and at that point the *simple bare bones* outline of the project will be advanced. The pivotal point is reached when the critical group in this focused thought is in harmony with the surrounding galactic environment, when it conforms to and within the universal laws. and becomes the intent of humanity. It is then that the victory is won, the victors will write the new scenario and, on request, advice is available to accomplish the manifestation of the new experience. Again, free will is the controlling factor. The advisors have available technology that surpasses any that is present on earth. These can and will be shared and abundant life will not mean tramping barefoot in the desert, unless the victors steadfastly choose that scenario. If mankind chooses to stubbornly remain within the present belief system and continue the current scenario, tramping barefoot in the desert will seem abundant indeed.

Is the above meant as a threat? No indeed! Simply how it is!

II-29

It is the responsibility of those accepting the information/knowledge contained within these messages to integrate it into the structure of their belief system. Simply put, that means to live it into wisdom by delivering the message to Garcia. Garcia is everyone who can and will receive the messages and in turn deliver the message of the new paradigm to more that will accept the mission. In this way, the expansive flow of creation is then at work laying the foundation for the new paradigm. Once the simple statement of purpose is conceptualized it will rapidly reinforce the network that will then already be initialized. When the victim consciousness is transcended, the statement of purpose will lead individual and group awareness to the next level; thus it must be as simple as the statement of "I/we/they am/are (a) human(s) becoming, help me/us/them to become!" What logically is the next level of awareness to be encompassed in order to arrive at the ability to conceptualize the skeletal format of the new paradigm? What words would empower the human consciousness to lift its lethargic self-awareness to resolutely desire to determine its own present and future individually and in unity? This simple powerful call to the infinite potentiality of creation that is at the magnetic center of the self-awareness of each human is waiting to be tapped. (Ask the level of awareness that focuses creation through awareness at the level of the solar system, or even the galaxy. These do exist. Ask *from* a point of awareness beyond the victim consciousness and there will be an answer.)

Once awakened to itself, self-awareness desires and searches for channels through which to express. This potentiality has been perceived and exploited through techniques of manipulation by governmental and religious leaders of the past and present. A new paradigm must transcend this in order to be a new paradigm. It is not necessary to conceptualize the new paradigm in completeness to understand its purpose. Clearly delineating the purpose is the next logical step in the process. The mind filled with clutter doubts its ability to conceptualize something new amid the confusion that reigns. However, once the cause and intent of the confusion is perceived and the decision to release the victim stance is made, the clutter moves into the background. The awareness becomes intrigued as latent triggers are activated that intuitively bring to the conscious mind the desire for freedom to live a self-determined existence.

It is important to comprehend that the center of self-awareness, that aspect of self that knows it exists, is the magnetic focus that attracts the body and all experience. It is a holographic microchip of creation. A holograph can be replicated from a tiny cell of the original. As the creation is to be venerated, respected and held in the highest honor, so the self-awareness to be held in equal veneration, honor and respect. This magnet of energy is focused at conception and clothes itself in a body to experience and when withdrawn, death of the body results. It is up to each to contemplate the creation and to shine the light of the understanding of it through this microchip of self-awareness outward by living life's experiences into wisdom. As this is done within the universal laws that do govern this process, the holograph of the creation is gradually expressed through each one to a greater and greater degree. It is creation thinking and through projected thought expanding and knowing itself. Creation is self-aware through its focused microchips mimicking its own process. As each self-aware living being grows through wisdom acquired, the experiences change in dimensional magnitude. To those who acquire much wisdom, much is required to continue the exponential growth. Living the creational adventure is much like reading a good mystery book. Once involved in the scenario, it is difficult to stop reading, and it is difficult to stop desiring to evolve. Once side tracked, the urge to continue on in the process keeps pushing the awareness onward down the same path. Because of this impetus to keep on keeping on, there are those who volunteer to aid and assist their fellow aspects of creation to again find the open ended track of experience. Creation is maintained and expands through volunteerism. That is how it is!

II-30

The evolvement of each focused self-awareness is dependent upon its ability to process the knowledge available into and through its flow of experience. The influence of those entities around it, that believe certain truths and experiences are the truth or ultimate experience, leads to entrapment and endless dead end ventures. The ability to experience knowledge acquired and experienced into wisdom is like laying stepping stones on a path. When an understanding is complete, then it is necessary to acquire the material to complete the next stepping stone. It cannot be done with exactly the same knowledge as the last one. It must include new material/knowledge. There may or may not be a bridge between what has been learned and the subsequent new information. New concepts may contain essences of more than one stepping stone. It is this apt analogy that has lead to the idea that evolvement equates to a "spiritual path". The significant perception of the visualization of this path is the understanding that the stones must be present and laid one by one before there can be a path. Further and important is the concept that the path lies not before each traveler, but ***behind*** him/her.

It is rare that the path behind any evolving awareness is a smooth upward spiral. The acquisition of knowledge and experiencing it into understanding and releasing it as complete and then opening to begin the process again does not usually lead easily to the ultimate goal. The conceptualization of that goal is literally too incomprehensible to be able to limit it into words. However, the magnetism of that goal draws all ultimately to return to it. There is no escaping its allure no matter how crooked the path of wisdom is laid in the process of the return. The view of the path of humanity on this planet as a whole over the past several thousands of years would find it curling abruptly into a circle. Mankind has continued to march around and around that circle with few able to intuit their way out of it and to continue their evolvement.

That circle now is a spiral downward as the recent human

experience is being lead into the lower vibrational activities of greater and greater violence and denigration of the body and awareness. The foundations of family and personal integrity are visually and audibly assaulted with dogma of truly evil intent. It must be remembered that the altered humans conceived religion for the worth while purpose of preventing self-annihilation. Its original intent and purpose was not to provide the path to evolvement. It did, however, contain and retain some of the teachings of the benevolent visitors. There have also been not so benevolent visitors who have observed the religious process as a field of opportunity to promote their own agenda of retaliation and revenge. By infiltrating and slowly developing their strategies, the true teachings have been deliberately adulterated and used to promote the circle brought about by the genetic alteration and to turn it into a downward spiral.

It is the purpose of these messages to set forth the truth of the dilemma of humanity and to put forth some of the essentials of its knowable cosmology. The messages contain the elements of a workable plan to allow mankind to create for itself the opportunity to leave the downward spiral path that has resulted from not only the genetic alteration, but from their stubborn refusals to accept the proffered help. This stubborn refusal to let go of the old and continue their victim stance has allowed them to fall prey to those who take advantage of that level of consciousness. The portion of the population that was drawn to and has intermingled with the not so benevolent interplanetary visitors at the moment has the upper hand.

First enough humans must awaken to the situation set to overwhelm them. Second enough must consider the possibility of the truths offered within these messages. Third enough must have the courage to discern these truths and <u>follow the sugges-</u>

tions. These shall then guide their fellow humans through this dangerous situation to the new paradigm and the return to the galactic family. Then earth's people shall be *welcomed* through out creation to walk and learn among their friends and to gather the material for the stones of their individual paths. The limited and frustrating existence that has been experienced has not been a total loss. The advantages that await shall be greatly appreciated.

Each step as outlined is critical. Each requires courage both individually and as a combined focus. What is the most challenging is accepting the concept that there will not be an army gathered together physically to encourage one another. This will be accomplished by individuals that within their own focus faithfully commit and follow through daily by delineating their intentional desire for and resolve to move through the chaos to come. These will know in their hearts at an emotional level that does not waver that what is desired exists and is manifesting even now as the desire for it is embraced and being conceptualized. The miracle of the new paradigm will be a gathering of individual foci through their intent upon the same purposeful symbolic agreement. This cooperative focus will, through the law of attraction, acting through application of the law of intentional creation, bring forth the intended new experience. These with sure confidence will trust the process and *allow* it to happen. Then balance and harmony will reign. The truth of the presence and power of the universal laws, stimulated by the cooperative combined foci, will be demonstrated. Through this demonstration much will be experienced into wisdom earned and wisdom learned. Humanity will then stand on the stepping stone leading out of the downward spiral and find themselves facing the opportunity of creating new stones of wisdom for their paths within the new paradigm.

II-31

The understanding gained through the reading this material, especially those that have contemplated and pondered it for the specific purpose of feeling if there is a resonance with the truth present, has changed each person's perspective. Knowledge once gained changes the reality through which the life process is viewed and contemplated. When the purposefully focused mind clutter is observed with the discernment of its intended design, the perception of current reality is different. Even if the observer chooses to ignore the truth that was considered as a possibility, the ability to blend again into the sleeping masses can never be accomplished. It remains in the background and circumstances and events will continue to trigger the awareness of the truth. In this way the seeds of change are planted and will begin at some point to grow and bear fruit. Those who reject the information before considering it at all will find the choice will be offered again before the project of the new paradigm is complete.

The message carriers must understand that even though many will reject the information, making the contact invokes the opportunity of a future choice. In the case of those desiring this information to be accepted by family and friends to whom there are emotional attachments, this should be a comfort. The second offering will usually be through another messenger, and is more likely to be accepted for two reasons. First, it has been heard before, and it is easier to accept on a logical level that does not have emotional triggers involved. In this way each may be prepared for possible rejection, but will also know that even when that happens, a contact link is established. The gift is given whether it is accepted immediately or at a later time. If not accepted at all, then the difficult lesson of allowance is to be remembered, for each has their freewill choice. There is also the possibility that as the scenario evolves; these skeptics may seek out the information. The focus of intent through blessing the individuals "for their highest and best good" or a similar invocation carries the energy of the creative flow of expansion. The expansiveness of this energy has created galaxies, solar systems, planets and beings becoming to appreciate the process. This energy is as powerful as it is subtle. The more relaxed and knowing the "intender", the more potent the result.

As the messages are circulated, accepted and contemplated, the law of attraction begins to draw and attract more people of like beliefs. Those who are awake are beginning to realize that there is little information that goes the essential step further to suggest a true solution to the situation. Certain survival preparations are necessary, but these do not offer resolution. This awareness is magnetic and invokes an answer to the question of "What can we do?" The viable answer that provides a cure and not just symptom relief is found within these messages. The way in which other suggestions for resolving the situation at hand may be measured is to consider whether they offer a cure or merely symptom relief. As with a disease of the human body, a symptom seldom indicates the entire cause of the problem. The symptoms now affecting the whole of the human population and the planet are so numerous as to make an overview difficult. Few have the time, or have the tenacity to come to a clear conclusion on their own. They depend on the media and other controlled opinion givers for their picture of the larger reality because it is purposely available for easy access. It is psychologically written to present only facets of situations and events so as to deceive the listener/observer and encourage the unconscious cooperation needed to complete the preparations for enslavement one cautious step at a time. As the time draws near, the puppet leaders become more impatient and careless, yet the masses still do not hear or see. Know that this also serves the implementation of the new paradigm project. Be patient and lay the foundation blocks steadily and with purposeful resolve. Join in small groups of like awareness and contemplate the wording of the purpose, pass the messages and ***know*** this is the process of thought thinking within the universal laws. The desire for this new experience is already attracting its energetic format. Trust the process! This project has the blessing of the planet and its inhabitants as a whole as its purposeful intent. That is a major plus for the insurance of its success. It does require purposeful resolve. Hang in there and do all that is necessary with passion and zeal. Contemplate standing on the first stone outside the downward spiral, knowing the possibilities available when there are moments of discouragement. Smile, you are on the willing and winning team!

II-32

As these messages are distributed and the number of people reading and assimilating the knowledge contained within them increases, the natural flow of the law of attraction allows the gradual increase of their magnetic appeal to bring more and more people to grasp the logical understandings offered by them. The wave of discontent and frustration that is rising within the mass consciousness is developing. A viable solution that does not require the sacrifice of the human body to accomplish the desired reversal of the situation surrounding the whole of the mass consciousness, is applying pressure and bringing this to a moment that serves as the impetus for the birth of the new paradigm. It is appropriate to caution the team to remember that "divine order" does not necessarily appear to operate in a sequential mode. It does require a simplistic definition of form, holographic in nature, and completes the necessary process in a variety of ways.

The key to completing this within the slower vibrational dimensions is holding the focus of the definition of form within the mind's eye for the long duration needed to allow the manifestation into observable reality. A critical number of foci holding this intention in place are needed, for each can or will do so for only a short period at time. Thus, if enough do this often enough and long enough, then the image is in continuous focus. This is the process of thought thinking at the level of necessity within the lower vibrational levels of what is called the 3rd dimension, or lowest dimension of human existence. It is the most difficult to transcend because the slow vibratory rate, at best, requires the focus to be held for manifestation to materialize. The lower the scale of the vibratory rates the longer the sequence and the more difficult it is for the mind to concentrate. The power of the competition of the planted clutter in the minds of humanity at the moment adds another ingredient to this already difficult situation.

It is thought that the lid is tightly shut and that it is impossible for the critical number of humanity to detect the net of deception, organize and transcend through the carefully laid trap into freedom. That in a nutshell, is the challenge. Can this "mission impossible" be accomplished? Is it possible for this sleeping giant to awaken, shake off the administered sedatives and arise into sufficient awareness to make the choices necessary? The ability to do so is present. The opportunity is now, for it will be a long time with much suffering before another will be available. It is said that mankind will give up luxury and all other manner of things and experience before he will give up the suffering that has been his lot for so long. Your christian religion teaches that

that suffering is holy and a bridge to the heavenly experience in the next lifetime by a "loving" god? Is this in any sense logical?

Each deception individually and the collective whole of them are incomprehensible to your cosmic brethren in that they defy logic. The whole of creation is logical. Logic is a wondrous balancing mechanism. The whole of the mass belief system for earth's inhabitants is so distorted through exploitation of the emotions that what is universal logic appears to be illogical and difficult to believe. In order for the new paradigm project to succeed, the messengers must digest the messages within the totality of their awareness and allow them to percolate through and to change their perception of not only who and what they are, but how they perceive creation. It will be necessary to allow the magnitude of misconception to resolve into a new basic perception and conception of the holographic, cooperating, interacting wholeness that focused them into being and holds them there in the freedom of freewill choice. Bondage is not the heritage of choice. It is giving up the basic framework of creation through the freewill choice of victim experience that has allowed this situation to regress to its present level. This is an opportunity to bring it to an end, and to progress into knowing again who you are and doing what you were designed to do. It is time to give up suffering and experience joy, bliss and ecstasy as the realities they are, not as fleeting moments or mythical goals for saints only. The ideal is neither abused children nor menacing warriors, but free fulfilled adults at home in a galactic world of adventure. Your lovingly concerned brethren offer here their proffered advice and promise of greater assistance if you but help yourselves first as citizenship within creation requires. It is hoped that each reader will ponder and consider the alternatives and choose wisely.

It is hoped that those who embrace the premise of these concepts grasp the dimensions for change that are available through the acceptance and incorporation of these suggestions. It is the incorporation of conceptual changes at individual and various inclusive group levels leading to global awareness that allows for the holographic requisite to be met. As the individual participates within the process, the consciousness transcends from personal experience expansively through groups arriving at the global dimension. Each and all then stand on a new platform to contemplate galactic experience. Through visualizing the expansion inherent in the sequence of necessary steps it is possible to comprehend a multi-dimensional process on going within a singular focused goal. Once this is experienced into wisdom, then it is available to be experienced in other situations for varied appropriate applications.

It is relevant to point out that the process is best learned before attempting to apply it in other situations. Rather like stringing pearls for a necklace, it is best to focus on one pearl at a time. In this case the pearl of the moment is the new paradigm. It is what must be held in focus, all else will then follow in due time. It cannot be stressed enough that scattering the focus was not the intent of this greater understanding. Stay focused on creating the new paradigm, then the joy of experimenting with this process will be splendid indeed. It is then that the focus shared between galactic family members will stand forth as intended.

II-33

Within the experience of the chaos that lies in the near future, the allowance of the experience will be a difficult hurtle for those that intend to focus the new paradigm through its initial stages of inception and birth it into manifestation. There will be difficult and discouraging moments for those who accept this mission, especially if there are no close companions to share the focus and encourage each other. Holding chosen simple symbols clearly in mind and drawing or seeing them displayed as frequent reminders will assist in holding the necessary focus. The symbols bring the focus to mind without the conscious effort of first identifying the focus and then convincing the intellect of its truth when the surrounding situation contradicts its rationality. The symbols are what might be called a "quick fix." Frequent reference to them on a continuing basis and allowing an emotional feeling to arise in anticipation of the coming new experience will bring immeasurable focused energy to the manifestation.

When this simple exercise is practiced with the discernment of its meaning in innumerable places on the planet in a continuous format, the manifestation is assured. If each time the symbol is focused upon, it is perceived as a flash of light or an electrical charge, the planet can be envisioned as literally lighting up with this new perception. This is an apt analogy and allows for consideration of the power held within the simplicity of redirecting purposeful intention through placing the attention on what is desired rather than what appears to be happening. It changes the control point from the observed to the observer that allows for empowerment of the individual observers. It further demonstrates the power of cooperation through unified commitment to a common goal. The fact that the goal is not defined in detail implies the process for the details do not dilute or scatter the focus. This project transcends merely identifying the problems and attempting to fix the symptoms for this in reality only adds to the problem as a whole. It provides the opportunity of experiencing aspects of the new paradigm as it is being created.

The parameters of the current pattern of life expression now being experienced must begin to shift in order for the new paradigm to be conceived and birthed into manifested reality. New parameters have been enumerated throughout these messages so that they might begin to filter into the minds of those reading, contemplating and discussing these concepts. The limited thinking of earth's inhabitants must change to allow for the flow of thought to move through their conscious awareness on a continuing basis. To simply exchange one box of concepts for a new box of concepts will not allow for participation within the flow of creation. This is not to say that the flow of conceptual thought does not proceed in an orderly fashion, for otherwise the flow would be experienced as continuous chaos and that is not a flow. Indeed periods of what might be termed chaos are experienced while letting go of one set of truths and accepting another that delineates the next set of experiences in the search for greater wisdom. How much chaos is experienced depends on how long the old set is retained before the necessity is to move on brings a breakthrough. If an openness to perceive and accept seemingly new concepts of truth is practiced, then the process proceeds with greater smoothness.

It is hoped that those who embrace the premise of these concepts grasp the dimensions for change that are available through the acceptance and incorporation of these suggestions. It is the incorporation of conceptual changes at individual and various inclusive group levels leading to global awareness that allows for the holographic requisite to be met. As the individual participates within the process, the consciousness transcends from personal experience expansively through groups arriving a the global dimension. Each and all then stand on a new platform to contemplate galactic experience. Through visualizing the expansion inherent in the sequence of necessary steps it is possible to comprehend a multi-dimensional process on going within a singular focused goal. Once this is experienced into wisdom, then it is available to be experienced in other situations for varied appropriate applications.

It is relevant to point out that the process is best learned before attempting to apply it in other situations. Rather like stringing pearls for a necklace, it is best to focus on one pearl at a time. In this case the pearl of the moment is the new paradigm. It is what must be held in focus, all else will then follow in due time. It cannot be stressed enough that scattering the focus was not the intent of this greater understanding. Stay focused on creating the new paradigm, then the joy of experimenting with this process will be splendid indeed. It is then that the focus shared between galactic family members will stand forth as intended.

II-34

The evolving consciousness within the holographic planetary system arises out of the individual conscious awareness, as it perceives itself within the whole. The perception of what that wholeness includes varies in accordance with what is experienced. Until the advent of the technological era these individual experiences were influenced by the belief system that was absorbed from the family environment followed by those acquired within expansion into larger group experience. Cosmology, the understanding of the how the individual fits into the perceived plan of the galaxy/universe, was taught by symbology within story, art and dance. This allowed for each to contemplate their place and encouraged each to quest to know and understand. With the advent of the printed word followed by graphic technology and the use of it for the manipulation of mankind into slavery, this process has been virtually lost. If the technology had been used to assist the individual to know and understand what truth is available rather than keeping the key information hidden or distorted, mankind would not be within the present dilemma.

Thus it is that these messages are given in the hope that the small amount of truth and wisdom within its pages will entice the reader/messengers to desire to again quest for understanding of who and what they are. This is not done, except by the few intent upon self-discovery, within the current planetary situation. This inherent right to know is denied from early childhood on through maturation as the present circumstances are now. Those in the more technologically advanced cultures are overwhelmed with misinformation and those in the less advanced cultures are existing at extreme poverty levels. It is difficult to wonder about a place in the plan of the cosmos when need of basic food and shelter are in the forefront of consciousness. Further, technology has been turned to cause the human body to literally self-destruct through weakening its foods with growing techniques, incompatible food combinations, genetic alterations to the plants, adding abrasive ingredients and cooking in fashions that alter the molecular arrangement of the foods. These are affecting the ability of the human body and the plants and animals to reproduce in perfection. The seriousness of the situation is realized by a few that attempt to spread the warnings. Without help from those with a great understanding of methods of regaining perfection, there will follow generations of imperfect bodies as a result.

Though it is the purpose of these messages to offer a plan for transcending the planetary dilemma, it is necessary that those who accept this mission fully understand that humanity on this planet is in direful straits that are worsening at a rapid pace. It is necessary that the end of this situation be reached soon, for as the damaged humans reproduce, the return of the next generations to perfection becomes more complicated as the mutations begin to scatter into dominant and recessive gene combinations. Within the generation of the acquired damage these imperfections are yet correctable. The evil of the plan to produce slaves includes these mutations, for imperfect bodies set the stage for belief of inferiority as well as the real affects to the physical brains and bodies. With the addition of technological implants the slavery would be virtually complete and provide far more control than those methods employed now.

It is not intended to place information in these messages to frighten the readers into buying into its plan. The overview would not be complete so that logical and intelligent decisions could be made if at least an encapsulated picture of the situation and circumstances that are present was not included. The truth of what has been stated above is available in book, magazine, web-site and radio. Portions of it are included in the media controlled programs, but go unnoticed. It is then in truth that it can be stated that they told you so and that you paid no attention. They knew that amid the clutter, few would put it together or pay attention to those that did.

Of further note is the fact that through the "United Nations" the military forces are being scattered through out the world. This is for the reason that many would not enforce the coming orders against their own people, but with the ethnic and national rivalries, could and will against those of other nations, cultures and particularly those of other religions. If the attention is placed only on the situation and circumstances that surround you at every turn then overwhelm is experienced and that is exactly what it is desired for those of you who are awakening. It is the reason there is no concern about their plans being revealed at this stage. That it is yet possible to gather a focus with power enough to thwart their plans even now does not occur to them. Thus, there is yet the "freedom" to implement project new paradigm. Shall we proceed?

II-35

It is through the application of the law of allowance that mankind will make the final step into the role of the rainbow "hu<u>man</u>". The archetype of the warrior that has influenced the shaping of mankind's experience shall at long last evolve into the ideal of the responsible cosmic citizen. It is perfectly possible to adventure in a role beyond the warrior. Only other warriors within the game of conflict welcome warriors. Those who have evolved beyond walking this dead end path do not welcome conflict back into their experience. The freedom to move freely among those of more refined development allows for more rapid advancement. As within a maze, eventually it is necessary to face the wall at the end and accept it as the end, and stay there, or to find the way back to the correct passageway. The new paradigm is a gift that will enable humanity to rise above the maze to see the true passageway and move quickly into it.

This will not happen without the necessary consciousness change and the period of focus required through the chaos of the demise of the current mode of experience that is based on competition and conflict. The desire for the new experiencing mode must become a passion that exceeds the inclination to stay within what is familiar. The realization that something far better waits at the closure of this experiencing mode must be real within the belief system and be strong enough to transcend the mass beliefs of not only millions, but billions. It is through the demonstration of the power of a combined human focus that *blends with* the wisdom of creation that each will know the truth. It is not to be found in resistance to the situation that exists on this earth plane, but in *joining with* that which is Truth that will bring forth what seems to require a miracle to accomplish. Unimaginable power will be tapped in this process. It simply requires changing the focus of the combined minds of a percentage of mankind. It is not a majority; it is an amazingly small actual number of humans on earth comparatively speaking, for these will blend with the flow that creates planets, stars, solar systems, galaxies, and more.

The process is simple. The complication is that it requires standing and turning into the face of what has been taught for generation after generation by doing it within each individual consciousness. It does not require face to face confrontation with those that continue to teach these untruths. Most do this in sincerity. It is through one to one contacts with those that already feel discontent with available knowledge at the deep levels of their personal awareness, that the mission is to be accomplished. There are more than enough that sense they are swimming upstream and are ready and willing to rejoin the flow of creation. They wait only to know how to accomplish this change. The archetype of the rainbow human calls to all for it is like a homing signal that perpetually sounds in the background of life. It is like the dinner bell ringing in the distance to come home to share refreshment and rest with family. In this case, humanity has wandered far from home and has some distance to cover, but it will arrive there sooner or later, and hopefully it will be sooner!

The focus has been at the very personal level for each messenger as each goes through the process of strengthening his or her understandings and resolve. It is not easy to commit to a project of this magnitude without establishing the intent firmly within the conscious mind. The mind and the feelings must be in harmony and balance in order that the resolve is of enough substance to hold firmly through the period of the shift in consciousness. That which is now new must have time to root and become the dominant viewpoint from which experiences are perceived and decisions made with discernment. An amazing number of life situations will suddenly take on new meanings. Habitual comments that fit certain situations will no longer be appropriate and there will be moments of wondering what is appropriate. There will be rethinking necessary requiring a transition period. There will be many returns to the messages to contemplate new meanings that were missed when first read. Truth is perceived within the understanding of the moment and is constantly refreshed as different experiences are contemplated and decisions are necessary for the discernment needed to establish new patterns of belief and behavior.

There is much to transcend in order that each may stand at the end of this chapter of the book of evolvement and contemplate not only a new chapter, but also a sequel. This will be done day by day and one mind change at a time. The biggest single change is the willingness to read, contemplate and find the personal truth within with the guidance of these messages. Beyond that, the steps are small and continuously lead onward to the goal of living the new ideal or archetype moment by moment. When the new archetype is embedded within the mass consciousness, the new paradigm will be birthed into infancy and the adventure will have begun in earnest. Then you may choose to walk hand in hand with your family again for you will have returned home for sustenance and companionship. A worthy trade off for giving up excessive competition, conflict and isolation.

II-36

Within these messages is embedded the psychological changes of heart and mind that are required to maintain the focus of the powerful aspects of experience that constitute the human evolving within the successive steps of its journey. The focused human awareness can be observed as a matrix or pattern of energy, for that is what each is in reality. Each cell contains an electrical charge, therefore if the charges are observed they would appear as a pattern of lights surrounded by a finer thought energy that is emitted as these pass outward from the being. Since all of creation in its basic form once beyond pure potentiality is thought, and thought thinks, then it may be concluded that the totality of the human thinks. Every cell of the human body thinks. It is how feeling is experienced. It is how a deep realization can cause what you call goose bumps to arise on the body, for the entirety of the body has agreed simultaneously on a new concept of truth. That is what sends some to a doctor, because there is a knowingness from within the body that has been emitted from the body cells into the finer thought energies that surround the body and the conscious mind has opened to receive the information.

The thought function is not confined to the brain. It is the totality of the human that participates in the thinking process. Feeling is a combination of thought processes by the cells of the body utilizing the pathways of the nervous system as you use telephone lines. But just as you receive TV and Cellular phone messages without the benefit of wires, so also the body has similar and far more refined capabilities. What is called intuition is an illustration of this more refined ability. It is a knowingness that takes place at a cellular level and registers in the awareness at varying degrees of understanding, depending on the belief system of the individual. The brain is designed to participate in a multitude of processes. It houses the most vulnerable and finely tuned of the endocrine glands. The precious secretions of the pituitary and pineal glands are the drivers of the human body/mind awareness. The brain is the switching station for the receiving and transmitting of the thinking process. The combined thought process of the body wholeness is gathered and focused through the brain mechanism that it may be exchanged between humans. However, it must pass through the belief system stored in the finer energies that surround the body and hold the belief patterns of not only the individuals experiences, but also contains the norms of the experience and belief patterns of the various levels of experience of the entire planet. One function of the brain is to register and read that information upon request. Thus when certain parts of the brain are stimulated, it reads not itself, but the stored data that is within the appropriate surrounding fine energy. Each human brings its entire history of existence with it stored in this incredibly intelligent energy that surrounds it.

This then explains one reason that humanity on this planet cannot enter the higher dimensions as it is now, for those beings are able to read the finer surrounding energy and know all there is to know about each one, every thought and intention. This is the source of what you call telepathy. How is this possible? It is the degree of activity of those two glands held within the brain, the pituitary and the pineal, that is the key to what you call "spiritual progress". The protection of these glands has been provided for by what is called the blood/brain barrier. Only very tiny molecules are able to pass through this barrier. Unfortunately for humanity at this time, crossing this barrier is now possible. Fortunately, there are those individuals who upon learning this are devoting great effort to get information out to make as many as possible aware. It is not only what is eaten, but also what is put on the body for cleanliness and other reasons that now contain destructive molecules that can and do cross that blood/brain barrier. These are causing great damage to the human brain as well as the rest of the body. For personal protection and the protection of the generations of the future, each messenger must become aware of these dangers and strive to find the safest available alternatives for themselves as well as to carry the message to others. There are alternatives available but it will require effort to search them out. It is important to know and to read what is within each before buying. It will be time better spent than in front of the propaganda tube.

Again, the focus is on the chaos rather than the goal, but the goal is of no benefit if there are not humans in wholeness to bring forth and enjoy the manifestation of the new paradigm of experience. Thus it is important that certain awareness be made particularly known. There is methodology in development that allows for the return of damaged DNA to wholeness without man made chemicals that are now being developed for that purpose. Beware of manmade intervention at these early stages. Nature has provided even this process for the preservation of the human in wholeness. There are indeed safeguards to protect humanity from self-destruction if it is studied within nature rather than pursuing the deliberately distorted guidance now being provided to the planners of enslavement. Though much is done in the competition/greed mode, it is underlain by the intentional provision of information that serves the enslavement purpose.

Each committed and focused member of the new paradigm project must practice discernment as the awareness of the picture begins as an outline and infills with information without becoming lost in the enormity and detail of the opposition's plan. It must be held in the background while the focus remains in place on the desired new paradigm. There will be quite naturally perusals through curiosity into the activities and plans of the dark ones, but these must be kept in perspective. The new paradigm must be held at the forefront of the focused awareness in order that it may manifest into its intended blessing.

II-37

The progression of the plan of the enslavement of humanity proceeds down its apparently inevitable path and mankind as a whole stumble along into the planned containment. It is difficult to include within these messages the information that it is necessary to be known without triggering fear. Yet fear is a most effective attention device and one that is planned to be used to the full degree of its potential to shock people into full awareness. Thus it is necessary that the plan for the new paradigm include utilizing this planned episode to its advantage. In other words, to divert this potential to fit within the plan to return humanity to its rightful place within the flow of creation. In order to accomplish this, there must be a core group of dedicated humans already awake and aware that has progressed through the potential fear and well in control of their reactive modes of behavior. In order to accomplish this, these must be able to transcend the planned response and quickly attain and retain the observer mode. Without this ability the capacity and competency to accomplish their mission that will be critical in that moment will be lost. As these who choose to become part of this plan make it a point to become aware of the plans, knowing it is a necessary component of the foundation upon which the birth of the new paradigm rests, it will allow the observer mode to be experienced into wisdom.

It will be easy to lapse into emotional reactions. However, the emotions are not to be the controlling factor. Creation is logical! Therefore in order to create, manifest into reality, a new paradigm of experience, those doing so must focus within logic. It certainly would not be logical to accomplish this by joining in the reaction that is intended by the enslavers. It then becomes necessary that there be a critical number of humans that rise above their natural inclination to be part of the intended mass reaction. In order to do this, these self-chosen individuals, singularly or in small groups will find it necessary to inform themselves of as much of the plan as possible. It will be necessary to embrace their feelings about these plans within the full knowledge that it is for the purpose of experiencing them into the purposeful wisdom of attaining the observer mode. It is through this observation ability that clear and logical decisions can be made in the moment not in retrospect when it is too late to accomplish what would have been possible in the precious moment lost.

The necessary information can be quickly learned within small discussion groups, for then the material available through the yet free flow of books, radio talk shows and the Internet can be researched and shared. It must be considered in the sharing that the plans that will be revealed are not as much the flat pieces of a jigsaw puzzle being fitted together, as they are a holographic puzzle. To illustrate that concept, there are wooden or plastic puzzles that create a sphere when placed together in the proper combination. These are more challenging than the flat puzzles and the intricacy involved illustrates the extent to which the planning of hundreds of years has been required to bring so many to such an effective point. It then will also illustrate all that can be negated through the simplicity of a plan that is devised within the flow of creation compared to one that is not. The complication facing the messengers of creation, which is indeed what each one committed to the new paradigm project is, is spearheading the consciousness change from victimhood to self-empowerment. It appears that only through desperate circumstances is the programmed human willing to give up deeply engrained beliefs though the experience of these beliefs has not brought to them the promised benefits. The practice and holding on to these takes them deeper and deeper in a downward spiral as they continue to fail to come to the realization that doing more of something that does not work will not make it work. Fear of the unknown locks them into unproductive behavior and illustrates the limitation of the victim consciousness that is being promoted to the maximum extent in this gross exploitation and degradation of the humans on this planet.

The question put to each reader of this material is whether or not to remain within the group headed to inevitably miserable deaths or enslavement as further mutated survivors, or to climb out on to the rock of observation. Once outside the mass awareness, that is truly a lack of awareness, then the mission becomes 2-fold. Gathering others willing to assist and together birthing the new paradigm. It is hoped that complexity will be avoided and simplicity will be strictly adhered to. It is complexity that scatters the focus. The more simple the focus, the more quickly the manifestation will occur. Further, those not resonating quickly to the information are to be released and allowed to remain where they are. The seed is planted, and those may yet follow at a more appropriate time. Never attempt to convince anyone. Like the folk hero, Johnny Appleseed, plant and move on to the next possible appropriate contact. Though the planter may not observe the result, result by the law of averages is assured. Releasing each contact to their own destiny is practicing the law of allowance. When it is unnecessary to defend the comfort zone, logic will often filter through the emotions and these may seek the planter out when it is obvious there is no necessity to defend their beliefs.

The desire for a solution to the intuitional awareness that all is not well is the field of opportunity for the entrance of a new archetype or ideal mode of experience. The coin of impending disaster has on its other side the opportunity for its opposite, what might be called heaven on earth in the christian idiom, a "hope" contained in all religions. It would seem that to be an instrumental part of providing earth's people the opportunity to experience this dream into reality would be a worthy goal. The choice lies within both logic and emotion as it is pondered carefully.

II-38

The opportunity that is offered within the scope of this project is multi-leveled or multi-dimensional in quality. It utilizes all levels or dimensions of the human aptitude in its focus of modifying the human perception of experience as those involved move through transcending from the present point of experience into the next level or dimension. Dimension is the preferred description for it indicates a more holographic concept. Level implies flat. The circumstances of manifested awareness in a human body are not experienced as level or flat. It is the addition of emotion that adds the dimensional quality to manifested awareness. (Indeed, there are those beings that do not have emotion as part of their experience and they desire greatly to add this dimension to their experience pattern.) It is important that the concept of dimension become familiar and be included in the conceptualizing of the new paradigm.

It is vital that the concept of the human body/mind/spirit also be made very clear. The awareness of existence within manifested experience is also dimensional. Certain of the animals have only the awareness of each moment. For them there is no past or future, only the moment. Since they are unable to retain those memories in detail, their survival is dependent on what is called instinctual awareness and tied directly to survival actions and reactions. Humanity has through domestication frustrated most of them greatly through neglect of their instinctual needs for at least partial freedom, natural varied diets and of late through providing creature comforts more appropriate for humans than fur/hair coated animals.

The human body is a composite of corrections to previous experiments that produced limited modes of physical experience. Through lessons learned, a model was conceived with the potential to evolve through multiple dimensions of experience. As the awareness changed patterns, the human body was designed to accompany that change. It was also designed so that the awareness could enter and leave a body. In other words, the awareness was not required to cease its existence if the body was destroyed through accident or inadequate maintenance. What you call disease is inadequate maintenance. The ability to enter and leave was a known requirement, for the potential of the human body is so limitless that its capabilities of adaptation are greater than units of self-awareness can comprehend in one focus of life experience.

It is important that the reader fully understand that the awareness is not the body, but is merely housed within the body during conscious awaking hours. It can and does sometimes leave the body during sleep, under anesthesia and traumatic periods of unconsciousness. The consciousness can be aware of this separation and can indeed train itself to leave the body intentionally. Some of those with this ability are being employed on a regular basis to intentionally visit particular people and events employing only their focused awareness/spirit, and then can and do report on these activities to those of the dark intent. Just as the physical body can be trained through gymnastics and other exacting physical sports to accomplish impressive feats, so also can the awareness be exercised and trained to do what most would consider difficult to believe. In this way each can begin to grasp that the "average human" on the planet is grossly unaware of its potential. The limitations of each are either self-imposed through acquired thought and belief patterns or through physical or mental limitations by genetic alteration/mutations. They are further limited by failure to maintain the physical body with proper exercise, breathing, whole foods and pure water.

Technology properly applied is a blessing to mankind. Technology guided by competition intended to create profit at the expense of one's fellow man results in greed. Through the law of attraction this intentional exploitation draws to those who do this their just due, or what might be called equal compensation. Realizations of the truth of what they are about that result in change of intention and action also allows for a change in the degree of experience drawn in accordance with the degree of change. It is important that it is clearly understood, *the laws of the universe work perfectly whether one is aware of them or not. They simply are!* To live in harmony within them is heaven on earth. Let us cooperatively strive to anchor the truth purposefully within the mass consciousness of mankind and birth the new paradigm into the human experience on this planet.

II-39

The concepts contained within the message information will begin with the first reading to change the perception of those that resonate with its intended solutions. It is apparent that the opposition's wars on poverty, crime, cancer and drugs have produced few positive results whatsoever. The conceptual purpose of war is to provide control over another group of humans, including their possessions. When this concept is applied to the wars on poverty, crime, cancer and drugs, it is possible to see how these fit the evil plans perfectly to manipulate and control from within more easily by gaining the consent of those that are the intended victims. These "intended" "good" intentions act as a magic trick to spread the focus of their intended purpose because they apply the law of attraction. By resisting these situations and circumstances through focus of fear thoughts and actions, large groups of humanity are drawn into the planned experience.

It can be concluded that this warring approach would not birth the new paradigm into reality. It is necessary to understand that a 90-degree turn or any other degree of turn short of a 180-degree turn to the opposite approach will not work. Those that make the decision to commit to birthing the new paradigm must make it their primary focus. What the opposing faction is focusing must be held in the peripheral vision. When their plans and actions are faced fully and embraced with fear it gives them the desired energetic support and aids them greatly in accomplishing their goals. It is important to be aware but to remain focused on the plan that fits like a hand into the glove of creation. The glove is simply awaiting mankind to place their hand within it.

Symbology will play an important part in the ability to hold the positive focus. These have been used for eons of time as a focus point that allows for individual understandings and interpretations *within* a basic concept. This calls forth freewill commitment rather than the resistance that comes forth when ideologies and dogmas are strictly structured. Self-awareness desires freedom and is drawn to a simple framework that allows for freedom within it. It was the simplistic framework of the USA that drew immigrants from the world over, for it offered freedoms that had been only dreamed of. The value of the opportunity within this framework, however, was not honored by succeeding generations. This golden opportunity has been bricked and barred in through laws and regulations that one by one weakened it. Greed and deceit are the mortar that holds these bricks and bars in place and its citizens in bondage. Slowly and cleverly accomplished, the majority of citizens adapt and barely notice as each generation accepts what is and the creeping changes introduced during each span of time.

The opposition is clever and insidious, patient and well organized and has advisors with great technology. The situation is serious indeed. Those who can comprehend the puzzle picture and its seriousness have the opportunity to choose the eventual outcome. The timing is now such that the occasion to even change the obvious outcome is long past. The sequence of events has reached the point of it being impossible to return to the previous opportunity by repairing the damage done. The plan within these messages, with widespread, purposeful and focussed commitment, can and will accomplish the desired goal. It will require transcending old belief systems and leaving them in the bag to be left in the hands of the evil planners. *These beliefs were designed by them to serve them.* The sooner all committed messengers realize and face this truth, the sooner the end of their planned scenario will come. The new paradigm will bring into being a new set of belief systems that serve humanity not enslavers. The tools of the current limited concept of government along with religion and war must be left behind in their bag of tricks. The magicians must be left to ply their trade among themselves *somewhere else.*

The above underlined phrase is a clue to what has been part of earth's past and present. It has been and is yet one of the "somewhere else" places. Has *all* of humanity been sent here because of past misbehavior? Not necessarily, many risk incarnations here for the opportunity to rise above (transcend) the negative behavior patterns and do succeed. Many do not and find themselves enmeshed in the circumstances of earth's current crisis. The successful manifestation of the new paradigm will change not only the future of most of earth's inhabitants but free the planet from this assignment.

It is necessary that each individual gives this choice serious consideration and makes their decision based on a careful logical and emotional basis. Both modes of experience will be actively required in tandem and synergistically. Each will support the other in times of doubt and frustration when all does not happen quickly enough or expectations exceed apparent results. The desire to rescue the suffering will be great and examples of victims will be paraded before you through every media means available for the purpose of keeping all locked within victim consciousness. The observer mode of allowance while the new paradigm focus manifests and brings the ultimate solution to their plight must be held securely at the forefront of the conscious awareness. If dropped, it must be quickly picked up. Looking at or recalling a meaningful symbol is the easiest way to regain the focus.

Will all that resonate and commit be able to retain their focus? The success of the project will depend on the consistent and the persistent. Each must look within themselves to determine if their evolvement and genetic adaptation is such that a commitment of this magnitude is possible, plausible and noble enough to find out if the traits of character necessary are available or not. It is certain that each one that commits will find out!

II-40

Although the messages appear to be focused toward requiring apparent super-human accomplishment, just as few ever bring forth the potential of the physical body, so also few explore the capabilities of the mental focus. The human becoming has the potential for expression in its physical, mental, emotional and spiritual aspects. It is has been the tendency of humans to pursue one or two of these aspects at a time. It is possible to accomplish a balanced development of all four within one lifetime. In this way each aspect supports the other within a balance that provides for a harmonious experience. This begins with a growing understanding and application of the universal laws, along with recognizing the various opportunities to insert variations of the statement "I am a human becoming, help me to become!" Inserting this statement into every applicable situation allows for experiencing the use of the mental focus to bring about a shift in the energies of a situation. This experience of the power of mental focus and the result of its focused use will allow each to experience knowledge into wisdom through actual self-empowerment. The use of this simple statement demonstrates the self-awareness taking charge of itself. Through changing the perspective within the self-awareness, in turn its perspective of the situation changes in the moment that it is happening. When the situation is perceived in a different way, it is changed. Each situation is as it is perceived. What appears as a single situation is as all participating perceive it, and is in reality multiple situations happening in a simultaneous moment.

The concept of time is in reality a no thing. It is an invention of the mind or ego recorder so that the events of experience can be perceived, analyzed and recorded. Inasmuch as the energy vibrates at such a slow rate at the 3rd dimensional level, this process is at such a slow rate that it appears to be in sequential order so that chaos is not experienced within the recording process. It is necessary that this be understood so that the concept of the new paradigm coming into existence when it is perceived is understood. When a sufficient number of mental foci desire to create this experience for themselves, it begins its manifestation process within the flow of creational thought energy. It literally already exists, it is just that the energy flow is so slow that it is not perceived or brought into the experience at the 3rd dimensional level until the sum of vibratory oscillations reaches the total necessary to manifest into realized experience. As each understands the density of earth's surrounding space and the slow rate of the humans experiencing in that space, it is possible to grasp the understanding of why it appears to be a time oriented process. In excessively simple terms, the thought process travels outward into the aqueous (fluid like) energy of the creational flow at a much more rapid pace than it returns as manifested reality. The focused thought process when fueled by emotion moves quickly through creational energy. As it leaves the dense field of energy, it becomes finer or vibrates more rapidly. It is the return trip, so to speak, in the manifestation process that slows in its oscillation rate. The law of attraction magnetizes the object of the focused thought that was "sent out into the creational field of energy" and it is returned to the point of origin. When the point of origin is vibrating at the slower rate, it appears within the sequential time orientation to manifest very slowly. If during this sequential experience, the focus is withdrawn or sufficiently weakened, the magnetic attraction process is aborted.

It is within this understanding that the concept of how the birthing of the new paradigm is entirely possible can be understood in rudimentary terms. It can also be understood that once the planners of the next "dark age of mankind" know of this plan and see it happening, the onslaught to stop it will be intense. It will require dedicated individuals and small rotating support groups to keep the necessary focus in tact in order to bring the manifestation into being. There will be no success if the focus become resistance. Allowance, difficult as it will be, must be practiced and the focus held knowing the new paradigm exists in the moment, not somewhere in the distant future. To know that without having it yet in the current experience will require sincere dedication. Experiencing this truth into wisdom will gift the humans who are able to do it into becoming at a vibratory rate unknown in the annals of evolving awareness.

Through the support of the changing of the cycles and those benevolent awareness points that not only know and understand the situation, but also offer all possible support, this project is guaranteed, *if* the necessary human quotient can be reached. The ground crew is in place and the opportunity is certainly available. Let us proceed.

II-41

The change in perspective that each acquires as these messages are read and contemplated is a process of exchanging old perceptions for new ones and climbing to the top of the rock so that each is discerning from a new and different viewpoint. With each new reading and contemplation, the viewpoint will change again. The belief system changes and allows the same printed words to stimulate a different recognition of the reality that each creates for him/herself. This is the natural flow of evolving life experience. The planners of containment continuously attempt to thwart this natural inclination through every control method possible. Government and media programming are their primary agents of control at the mental level. Fear is their primary tool at the emotional level. War and induced disease that goes hand in hand with destructive medical treatment are the control mechanisms at the physical level. That which controls the spiritual level of experience and interacts within the other three levels is religion.

The focus of religion is to contain and prevent the developing human awareness from reaching the goal of evolvement because its methodology is designed to hold the goal always beyond the reach of present time. Humanity has been fooled into believing a total contradiction. What is called reincarnation is denied yet reward for a life of suffering and sacrifice is to be attained after death or possibly by future generations. Where is there logic to be found in this concept? The cosmos positively could not exist if it was not logical! The universal laws that underpin all that is manifest are absolutely logical! Therefore the understanding of the cosmology of humanity must be logical in order that mankind may progress *within it, right now!* The planners of enslavement have it so easy when humans desiring evolvement are contained within the house of religion with its illogical and contradicting edicts that are sold into belief on "faith". Buying illogical concepts can be likened to padlocking the doors and windows of the prison on the inside and sliding the keys out under the door to the jailers. It's like asking the wolf to guard the sheep. Are all concepts within religion wrong? Certainly not! Much truth is contained within the tenets of all religions, but many distortions and outright fabrications are carefully included within each and every religion. These have been deliberately placed there to deceive and control.

At the beginning of these messages it was stated that the "God thing" was not a hoax. This is so; it is just that the perception of what "God" truly is has hopefully changed through these messages. Humanity has been deliberately guided to personify to identify. In reality, that which it has been led to personify is potentiality expressing into creation. The personality of this process is with each self-awareness, not an all-powerful outside being. The outward expression of potentiality through the creational process is to expand or separate the energy into self-aware units and all that is necessary for it to recognize and revere its own potentiality and discover how to empower itself. At that point, the return trip becomes the opposite of that process. It is a gathering process. The law of attraction draws these separate self-aware units into groups of awareness that "enjoy" pursuit of like or common focus that reveres the creation as a wholeness. These then become larger units of focus while yet maintaining their individual awareness. Evolvement becomes a joyful gathering of momentum for there is agreement and cooperation, not competition or friction.

It can now be apparent that the victim consciousness does not fit the above criteria for the return trip. The enslaving consciousness does not fit the above criteria either. Both vibrate at the lowest rate of human existence. Those within the "upper echelons" of the enslaving consciousness have found the humans on earth a most vexing group with which to cope. They have since "manufactured" a more satisfactory slave pattern. The emotions were left out of the design; it is easily programmed; the vibratory rate is below the possibility of consciousness evolvement; the rudimentary thought process is slow, as is the ability to adapt. The cost in resources to maintain them is very low, as there is no reproduction to control. Cloning reproduces them when conveniently needed. Humanity does offer something the new slave does not. Challenging entertainment!

Does that please you to know that your victim consciousness rates as challenging entertainment? I would think not. It is time to bring an end to this scenario and to write the script that will bring freedom and the conclusion to the "long suffering" that this branch of humanity has allowed itself to endure. It is time to become the winning team. It is time to claim the hoped for carrot offered by the devised religions of the enslavers. It is appropriate to birth the new paradigm now. It has been more than earned.

II-42

The approaching period of chaos has been mentioned in the previous messages. What this process might look like in detail has not been discussed. It is difficult to do this since what manifests and to what degree will be determined by the acceptance or rejection of the new paradigm concept and by who and how many. In order to delve into this area, it is necessary to consider that these messages are for the express purpose of empowering humanity to transcend, move through the current and approaching events to a new level of existence. This cannot be done if the attention is focused on the events that are now and will increasingly surround each and all. Fear is so engrained in the psyche of earth's inhabitants that it takes little to trigger it. It is not the purpose of these messages to engender fear as it is a mighty tool for dis-empowerment.

Understanding why "god allows this branch of humanity to suffer" is impossible to understand without encompassing the workings of the law of attraction. Victim/oppressor consciousness is two sides of the same coin. Existing at the lower scale of the vibratory range of manifested life experience; the magnetic attraction of the two is extremely strong. As the evolving consciousness strives to experience knowledge into wisdom it returns again and again to achieve freedom from this particular trap. The range of experience traverses between the two modes of expression. Each has experienced both within various levels. The planetary mass consciousness not only contains this mode of experience, but also indeed attracts it from other solar systems within the galactic whole. Thus earth indeed has outsiders contributing to this current era of experience. The time span of outside involvement of what you call extra terrestrials when read within a sequential scenario has been thousands of years. It has been for a long enough period that some of those extra terrestrials have evolved beyond that mode of experience and are now committed to correcting the results of their previous involvement with the people of earth. Inasmuch as they have transcended the victim/oppressor mode, it is within their wisdom to aid humanity if humanity will only accept the help available.

It is therefore with trepidation that the planned scenarios of the remaining oppressors/enslavers are mentioned within this focus. Since much material is available on these subjects, it is up to individuals to review the information available on radio talk shows, their web sites, books, magazines, newspapers and various conference/conventions that are available. It is extremely important that the shocking information available from these sources be processed ***through*** the individual's awareness. To remain stuck in the trauma of this knowledge will be fatal not only to the individual, but to the new paradigm project. The new paradigm is the only available pathway with success possibilities through this dilemma. Making such preparations as are appropriate for these possibilities is the most logical approach rather than simply continuing to process the information in panic and trauma. Promptly making simple appropriate plans and preparations through logical thought by listing and completing the suitable steps to be accomplished will not only relieve the trauma, but will bring forth the empowerment that transcends the feelings of victimhood these events were designed to engender.

The law of attraction works! That the USA and other countries have supported the attacks on the Moslem countries of the Arabs, and others draws the likelihood of the similar experience of being attacked. The media has given all forms of illogical reasons for these attacks that were not officially sanctioned by the elected representatives but were allowed with their consent and the foolish consent of the people as a whole. Discernment was left to representatives whose influence is peddled and coerced into compliance. To cry, "I/we didn't know," means nothing to the dead, dying and miserable people experiencing the situation that has been foisted on them. They are the victims and "you foolish ones" are the perpetrators by default and must by the law of attraction receive your just due. It will not be pleasant. What can you do to change it? Change your mind and withdraw your consent to these actions within your own consciousness. Open your eyes and ears to the deceptions that surround you and vow to create a new experience for all living on this planet.

There is only one race on this planet, the human race. The varieties in appearance and belief systems are "no things." The extraterrestrials are visitors who have no desire to live here, only to enjoy the adventure of continuing your enslavement. They are fully aware that the planet cannot long endure the over population that they have encouraged so that they could play at their war games and perfect their tools of annihilation. To them humanity and earth are like the virtual reality games your children in large and small bodies' play. It is long past time to wake up and grow up into your responsibility to end their game. Welcome to the real world that now surrounds you and is about to overwhelm you unless you act now.

II-43

The clarion call of these messages is formulated to reach into the very center of each heart and mind to resonate there. It is intended to be an internal process that will enable each one embracing the possibilities contained within them to establish a vantage point from which to gauge their progressing personal transition. If each will consider the changes in their views of the world events as they are reported now and as they were perceived a few weeks ago, a considerable difference in the ability to discern the magician at work should be possible. The understanding of the meaning of self-empowerment within the personal experience and relationships should also be apparent. The consideration of this might be approached as the difference between submissive, assertive and aggressive. It is the through application of the universal laws that balance and harmony is achieved, a middle ground of experience. Once this is experienced it becomes easier to realize when one leaves this balance toward one or the other of the polarities. It is taught in the current media/religious foci that "goodness" is the ideal. Balance is not found in the extreme of either polarity. It is through learning to discern where in the process each experience is or is leading in the play between the polarities that allows for wisdom to be attained.

The new paradigm will come into manifestation when a sufficient quota of humans on the planet identifies with its tenets. These will focus its becoming without the aggressiveness of an enslaver that would force its ideals on his/her fellow humans or the submissive victim that would purposefully refrain from participation assuming that others will accomplish it for them. The ideal participant will employ the universal laws of attraction through purposeful intent to manifest the new paradigm, actively sharing the concepts and allowing the process to unfold by holding the intent assertively within the consciousness. The focus will remain steadfastly within their awareness as the world and personal events move through their chaotic process of dismantling what now exists to allow the new to manifest. Unfortunately, the new cannot superimpose itself over the top of the present firmly held belief systems. The combined present belief systems hold the current disastrous stream of events in place. The belief in the repetitions of past experience of war, pestilence, disease and painful deaths as the proper end to a lifetime of victim/sacrifice for a future reward is rigidly held and constantly supported by the planners of another round of their virtual reality games.

It is through these simple messages that those of genuine concern are reaching out to counter the focus of literally thousands of years of deliberately ingrained manipulative programming into the individual and collective psyche of humanity. It is a very large expectation that is being placed in these messages in this endeavor to reach those who are at a state of evolvement to resonate with the truths contained within them. The realization of the futility of continuing on in the age old pattern of allowing others to write all the rules of the game is the trigger that brings forth the emotion and commitment to become a part of the momentum for moving on through to a new goal.

Just as several individuals can participate in a single event and each perceive and experience it differently, so also can a multitude of perceptions of what the new paradigm experience will be for each encompass the same definitive goal and accomplish that purpose. When the new paradigm is birthed, indeed each will experience it uniquely. If it were to be a totally defined picture it would again become encapsulated and enslaving. Within the laws of the universe, what you term ethics and morality are limited understandings. Within the higher dimensions, which is the purpose of leaving the current lesser vibratory experience through the new paradigm, it is possible for each to perceive the purposeful intent of all. This is not necessarily in detail at the lesser vibratory levels. Therefore dishonesty and aggressive intent is known and those with that level of intent find only those of similar intent to interact with. If there are no victims and only a group of aggressors to interact with, there is no game. It is to be expected that those ingrained thought patterns will show up in the beginning, however they will soon fade away as they are recognized. Do upper level dimensions lack challenge? No indeed! The challenges become subtler and even more rigorous to discern. Experience in the higher dimensions is not a boring "heavenly" evenness. The adventure of self-contemplation and growth becomes more and more interesting and the rewards more desirable. There will be no regrets for giving up the current belief systems and mode of experience, of that each can be absolutely sure.

The call for study, contemplation, commitment and follow through by defining the purpose and spreading the concept now is unfolding before each reader. It is doubted that any who are not seriously contemplating the process and anticipating the possibilities of the future of new experience will have reached this point in the messages. Both the logical and the emotional aspects resonate and the shift in consciousness is happening. Even those few that do turn away will not be able to return to their previous perspective of the current situation as it progresses toward the planned dark and dramatic shift. Those who do not choose to actively participate can yet share by simply holding the idea of the possibility of the time of the reign of the rainbow man arriving now. Legend has it that the first people on the planet climbed up out of the earth through a trapdoor. The rainbow man archetype is right now loosening the latch of the trapdoor that will allow his entry into the next level of manifested experience. It is time for this to happen!

II-44

The power of subtle thought when focused through the converging point of mutual agreement by a group purposefully representing a whole for the highest and best "good" of that whole is quite beyond the ability of the limited 3rd dimensional mind to comprehend. There is now documented evidence of the power of prayer in the recovery from illness when it is focused by doctors, nurses, friends and families for the "good" of the patient. The dynamic potential that is tapped is the *agreement* held within the focusing group's desire to bring forth the highest and best good for the person. The desire is usually limited to the person returning to an apparently "healthy" state. However, that is not always the true highest and best "good" for that person, since the purpose of the lifetime is usually unknown to the person and to those attending them, so it is best to leave the focus open. Further the person themselves may have already placed their decision as to their future into the flow of creation. Again this brings us back to the concept of thought thinking. The flow of creative energy that focuses each individual into manifestation to begin with and then maintains them in focus is intelligent thought thinking and is totally aware of what the highest and best good is in every instance *when it is directed to think within that concept.*

Self-aware consciousness is manifested thought aware of itself within its manifested surroundings. It is creation checking itself out for the purpose of knowing not only itself, but investigating its abilities to manipulate its potential to experience and know itself to a greater extent. Each of you are creational thought engaged in this marvelous experiment. You are intelligent thought surrounded by the potential of intelligent thought. The only way you can be controlled is to allow yourselves to believe you are something you are not. You must be convinced to believe you are something you are not. You must be convinced that you are powerless and subject to the will of others, thus a victim.

The intelligent thought that surrounds you is subject to your intentional will to direct it. If you fail to give it direction, it merely supports whatever direction someone else gives it regarding you. Thus through induced ignorance humanity has given consent to being manipulated. The most effective method for literally stealing your power has been through the diversion of the use of that power by convincing you to direct it outside yourselves to an unknown and little understood source, called "God". All power is vested in this vague unknowable entity that may or may not redirect the energy that is given to it back again to the worshipping requester. This is further diluted if the energy must first be directed through a "priest" like entity, who then directs it to the "God" and requests it to be returned to you. The point being, it is your power to direct as you see fit. You are the singular focus of creation experiencing as you. The bible contains a quoted question that reads something like "know you not that you are gods?" Indeed you know it now!

Learning to direct this power in *harmony* with the laws that under lay or support the wholeness of the flow of creation is the lesson to be accomplished. This cannot be effectively achieved unless the concept is known and accepted so that it may be practiced through experience into wisdom. Humanity on this planet is experiencing what results when the power of this energy is purposefully misused to restrict the evolvement of others for distorted experimentation. These entities are learning only how and to what extent others can be limited and manipulated into sacrifice and suffering. Observing is not experiencing into wisdom. Humanity is learning that sacrifice and suffering only brings more of the same. It is time to awaken and realize that continuing on the same path will only continue the pattern. In order to change this experience, the current pattern must be acknowledged and a new pattern conceived to replace it.

It may be difficult to accept that what has been taught for generations upon generations has been deliberately corrupted and given to you as truth in order to deceive and manipulate the entire population of a planet. It is more difficult to conceptualize a group focus that is so distorted as to spend eons of sequential time in the game of doing this dastardly deed. It is only necessary to accept it as what it is and resolve to withdraw your permission to be one of their plastic play pieces that bends and twists to fit their desires. It is the time now to take back your right to self-determination of your own present and future. This process leaves you not with less, but with more. You know in truth who and what you are. You now have a process in which to acquaint yourself with your inherent right and power to determine your own path. Leave the future of those who would enslave to the law of attraction. The key to their future is your withdrawal of approval and cooperation. In the moment in which their intense control focus is broken, the energy shifts for them also. Knowing this is enough. Do not spend time even considering their future. Be only concerned with creating your own. It is task enough to occupy each and all of you for some time to come.

Now is an excellent time to begin. Does a new future require that every aspect of your current experience be left behind? Not necessarily, but each must be considered carefully so that it fits in the wholeness that serves the evolvement of all. It is best to begin with the statement of purpose, then a simple framework that can be "painted" in with what is appropriate, remembering what is appropriate for one is not what may be appropriate for all. The application of the universal laws allows for diversity in harmony. A worthwhile goal to remember. If each is responsible for their individual intentions and actions all will come together in amazing coordinated cooperation. Within the true realization of time *there is only now.* The past is over and the future is yet to manifest as "the nows" pass into the past. The dream of the new paradigm begins now and continues now!

The following short list of books will introduce the reader to the awareness that the truth of the deceptions that have been perpetrated on the planetary citizens of earth is known and has been researched prior to these messages. The ancient records that have been found and more or less accurately translated have revealed much to support the hypothesis briefly mentioned in this book. Chronological information of the activities leading up to the present support the picture of continuing enlargement of the long standing plan for planetary violation. The information in the books listed below should be read with discernment for each author has made their own interpretations, often based on the opinions of others, and come to their own conclusions. These do not necessarily agree with each other or the information within the messages. It is for each to find the confirmations and contradictions within them and to come to their own conclusions. Much more data is available to be found if diligent research is initiated. However, research and reading for verification should not divert those committed to manifesting the New Paradigm of experience from their focus.

Handbook for the New Paradigm, Vol. I — ISBN: 1-893157-04-0

Becoming, Vol. III — ISBN: 1-893157-07-5

Conspirators' Hierarchy: The Story of the Committee of 300
by Dr. John Coleman — ISBN: 0-922356-57-2

Humanity's Extraterrestrial Origins
by Dr. Arthur David Horn — ISBN: 3-931-652-31-9

Gods of Eden by William Bramley — ISBN: 0-380-71807-3

Lifting the Veil by Jon Rappoport — ISBN: 0-939-0400-5-0

The Secret of Light by Walter Russell — ISBN: 1-879605-10-4

The Spiritual Laws and Lessons of the Universe
Lord Michael, St. Germain, Sananda & Druthea — ISBN: 0-96-40104-6-1

The Thirteenth Tribe by Arthur Koestler — ISBN: 0-394-40284-7

The Talmud of Jmmanuel by Rashid, Meier, Green & Zeigler,
ISBN: 0-926524-12-7

Celestial Teachings
(Explores the authenticity of the Talmud Jmmanuel)
by James W. Deardorff — ISBN: 0-926524-11-9